T0323787

DOCUMENTS OF
LADY JANE GREY

DOCUMENTS OF

LADY JANE GREY

NINE DAYS QUEEN OF ENGLAND, 1553

James D. Taylor, Jr.

Algora Publishing
New York

© 2004 by Algora Publishing.
All Rights Reserved
www.algora.com

No portion of this book (beyond what is permitted by
Sections 107 or 108 of the United States Copyright Act of 1976)
may be reproduced by any process, stored in a retrieval system,
or transmitted in any form, or by any means, without the
express written permission of the publisher.
ISBN: 0-87586-334-5 (softcover)
ISBN: 0-87586-335-3 (hardcover)
ISBN: 0-87586-336-1 (ebook)

Library of Congress Cataloging-in-Publication Data —

Documents of Lady Jane Grey, nine days Queen of England,
1553 / compiled by James D. Taylor Jr.
    p. cm.
Includes bibliographical references and index.
ISBN 0-87586-334-5 (pbk.: alk. paper) — ISBN 0-87586-
335-3 (hard: alk. paper) — ISBN 0-87586-336-1 (ebook)
1. Grey, Jane, Lady, 1537-1554. 2. Great Britain—Kings and
rulers—Succession—History—16th Century—Sources. 3.
Queens—Great Britain—Biography—Sources. I. Taylor,
James D., 1958-

    DA345.1.D9D63 2004
    942.05'3'092—dc22
                                            2004017645

Printed in the United States

ACKNOWLEDGMENTS

I wish to thank the University of Michigan at Ann Arbor and the British Library, whose vast holdings, resources and patient staff have made this work possible.

I also must thank the staff at the Pitts Theology Library at Emory University; the Bodleian Library and Ashmolean Library at Oxford; the William Andrew Clark Memorial Library at the University of California; the Folger Shakespeare Library; the Special Collections Department at the Alderman Memorial Library at the University of Virginia; and Charlene Berry at Madonna University for her spiritual support throughout this project.

Thank you all.

Genealogy of Lady Jane Grey

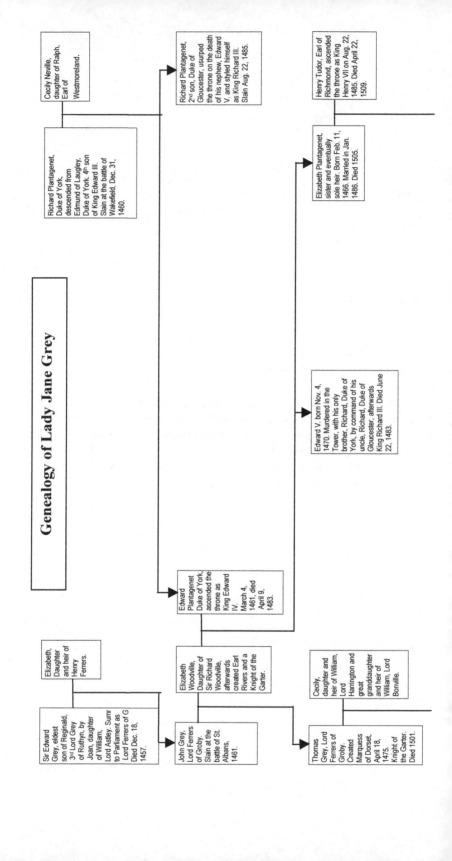

Cecily Neville, daughter of Ralph, Earl of Westmoreland.

Richard Plantagenet, Duke of York, descended from Edmund of Laugley, Duke of York. 4th son of King Edward III. Slain at the battle of Wakefield, Dec. 31, 1460.

Richard Plantagenet, 2nd son, Duke of Gloucester, usurped the throne on the death of his nephew, Edward V. and styled himself as King Richard III. Slain Aug. 22, 1485.

Henry Tudor, Earl of Richmond, ascended the throne as King Henry VII on Aug. 22, 1485. Died April 22, 1509.

Elizabeth Plantagenet, sister and eventually sole heir. Born Feb. 11, 1466. Married in Jan. 1486. Died 1505.

Elizabeth, Daughter and heir of Henry Ferrers.

Edward V. born Nov. 4, 1470. Murdered in the Tower, with his only brother, Richard, Duke of York, by command of his uncle, Richard, Duke of Gloucester, afterwards King Richard III. Died June 22, 1483.

Edward Plantagenet Duke of York, ascended the throne as King Edward IV. March 4, 1461, died April 9, 1483.

Sir Edward Grey, eldest son of Reginald, 3rd Lord Grey of Ruthyn, by Joan, daughter of William, Lord Astley, Sumr to Parliament as Lord Ferrers of G Died Dec. 18, 1457.

Elizabeth Woodville, Daughter of Sir Richard Woodville, afterwards created Earl Rivers and a Knight of the Garter.

Cecily, daughter and heir of William, Lord Harrington and great granddaughter and heir of William, Lord Bonville.

John Grey, Lord Ferrers of Groby. Slain at the battle of St. Albans, 1461.

Thomas Grey, Lord Ferrers of Groby. Created Marquess of Dorset, April 18, 1475. Knight of the Garter. Died 1501.

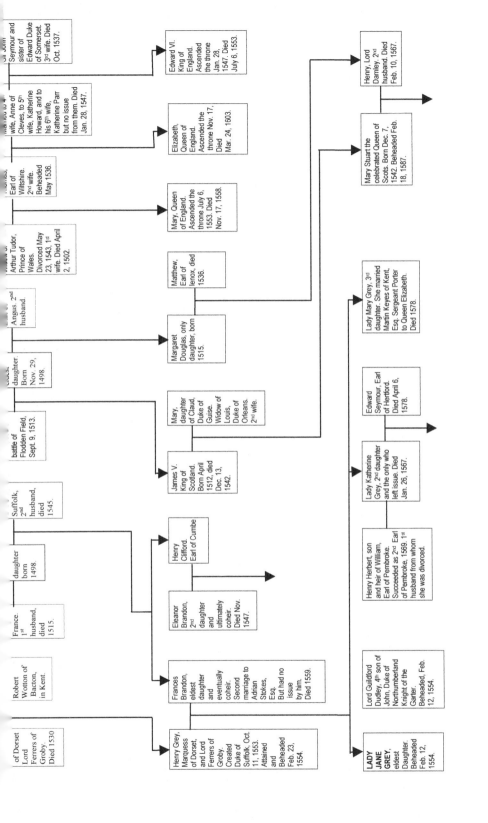

TABLE OF CONTENTS

PREFACE

I undertook this project in 1995 because of my frustration after reading two colorful books about Lady Jane Grey that embellished a few well-known facts and contradicted one another. Curiosity prompted further investigation over the next seven years and I reviewed the available sources of information and literary remains from the period only to encounter further inconsistencies.

Several factors, such as the literacy of the scribe or printer, may account for the inconsistencies. One important factor was the condensing or summarizing of information done by early authors. I chose to compile all the known letters and documents by or about Lady Jane Grey and present them together for the first time in this volume. I have chosen to use modern versions of some of the letters, for the sake of easier readability. The original letters were written in High Renaissance English and use many archaic words and terms that can be very difficult for readers without special training. The letters and documents contained in this volume were compared to the original material, when available, and best represent the primary material. In the majority of these, the only difference between the original and the edited version is limited to changes to a few words. To avoid burdening the text with extensive and redundant footnotes, parenthetical notes are included in reference to the bibliography.

Fortunately, those years of research produced occasional rewards. Among the gems I uncovered, and perhaps the most valuable, is a collection of letters that William Lane purchased from an unidentified source while he was at the Minerva Press, possibly during the year of 1790 or 1791. Though these letters are not dated, I feel confident that I was able to place them within a narrow margin by correlating well-recorded events in history and some of the events indicated in the letters. These letters provide particular insight into the turbulent Tudor period.

My intent is to provide a complete and accurate study of Lady Jane Grey's short reign through primary and secondary sources and to stimulate new questions in the mind of readers. Each letter or document has been reviewed at its original source level, translated from another language, or transcribed and presented in that form. I have also indicated the primary source for each document, and noted any supporting source or sources if available or known.

— James D. Taylor, Jr.

CHAPTER 1. PRE-REIGN PERIOD

Lady Jane is very often overlooked in historical studies of England, as many do not recognize the fact that she did reign as Queen of England. Though her reign lasted only nine days, her tale provides insight into the ongoing contest for control of England and the war that was waged, in which masses of soldiers often played a smaller role than the scions of top families who were pressed into service and gave their all.

The information contained herein about Lady Jane's ancestry has been transcribed for the most part from the numerous editions of English history by Nicholas Harris Nicolas, including the ancestral tree which I have corrected in minor ways to reflect new information that has appeared since it was originally published in 1825.

Lady Jane's lineage was certainly a source of great pride. Her father's ancestral tree was one of the kingdom's oldest, with several ennobled branches. Rollo of Fulbert was Chamberland to Robert, Duke of Normandy, and obtained the castle of Croy in Picardy, from which territory he adopted the surname DeCroy, later altered to DeGrey. According to many writers of the period, his grandson, Sir Arnold DeGrey, accompanied William the Conqueror into England

and was seated at Rotherfield in the county of Oxford soon after the conquest.

The first member of the family to be noted was Henry de Grey. Richard I granted him the manor of Thurrock in Essex; this was confirmed to him by King John in the first year of his reign, along with a charter of license to hunt hare and fox in any lands belonging to the Crown except the King's own demesne parks. From the younger sons of this Henry sprang the numerous Grey families conspicuous in the baronage and history of England.

John, the second son, Justice of Chester from 1233 to 1248, was the father of Reginald DeGrey, also Justice of Chester, whom Edward I rewarded for eminent service by a grant of the castle of Ruthyn. In the 23rd year of Edward's reign, Reginald was summoned to Parliament. He died in 1308, and was succeeded by his son and heir, John, who was twice married. The issue of his first wife continued the baronial line of Grey de Wilton, which continued in uninterrupted descent and honor for over three hundred years. In 1614, the line failed to produce a male heir, resulting in the forfeiture of the dignities of the house by the attainder of Thomas Lord Grey of Wilton (who died in prison, sentenced to death for his role in a plot against the king).

John Lord Grey's second wife, Maud, daughter of Ralph, Lord Basset of Drayton, bore a younger son, Roger, upon whom Grey bestowed the castle and lands of Ruthyn. He sired a house equal in splendor and reputation to that of Grey of Wilton and was summoned to Parliament as Lord Grey of Ruthyn in the seventeenth year of the reign of Edward II. He died March 6, 1353, leaving his second son Reginald as heir, since John de Grey, the eldest son and a personage of considerable consequence, had already passed away. A Sir Edward de Grey married Elizabeth, daughter and heiress of Henry Ferrers, eldest son of William Lord Ferrers of Groby. Henry died in his father's lifetime, and since Elizabeth inherited the baronetcy, her husband was summoned to Parliament in her right as Lord Ferrers of Groby in 1448. He died December 18, 1460, with John Grey as his heir.

We now arrive at an interesting point in Lady Jane's ancestral lineage: the marriage of John Grey, Lord Ferrers of Groby, to Elizabeth Woodville, daughter of Sir Richard Woodville, later created Earl Rivers. John Grey died in the battle of St. Albans in 1461, leaving Elizabeth a widow with two sons, Sir Thomas and Sir Richard Grey. At this point, Elizabeth attracted the attention of Edward Plantagenet, Duke of York, who ascended the throne as Edward IV on March 4, 1461. She eventually joined him on the throne as his queen, and bore him two children, a son, Edward V, who was murdered in the Tower, and a daughter, Elizabeth.

Elizabeth has been the subject of many an author's pen. She was Lady Jane's great-great-grandmother, as well as the ancestress of England's Tudors after the death of Richard III — facts that justify the inclusion in this book of a document that has escaped general notice.

The misery Elizabeth endured later in life began when Henry VII seized his mother-in-law's possessions, perhaps out of jealousy. She retired or, more likely, was confined to the Abby of Bermondsey, where she died. Her will speaks vividly of her love for her children and her sorrow that she could leave them little beyond her personal belongings.

In Dei nominee. The Xth day of April, the year of our Lord God, MCCCCLXXXXII. I Elizabeth, by the grace of God, Queen of England, late wife to the most victorious Prince of blessed memory, Edward IV, being of whole mind: seeing the world so transitory, and no creature certain when they shall depart from hence, having Almighty God fresh in mind, in whom is all mercy and grace, bequeath my soul into his hands, beseeching him of the same mercy to accept it graciously; and our blessed Lady, Queen of comfort, and all the hole company of Heaven to be good means for me.

Item, I bequeath my body to be buried with the body of my lord at Windsor, according to the will of my said lord and mine, without pompous entering [without a pompous funeral] or costly expenses done thereabouts.

Item, Whereas I have no worldly goods to do the Queen's grace, my dearest daughter, a pleasure with, neither to reward any of my children according to my heart and mind, I beseech Almighty God to bless her grace with all her noble issue, and with as good heart and mind as is to me possible, I give her grace my blessing, and all the aforesaid my children.

Item, I will that such small stuff and goods that I have, be disposed truly in contention of my debits, and for the health of my soul, as far as the[y] will extend.

Item, If any of my blood will any of my said stuff or goods to me pertaining, I will that they have the preferment before any other, and of this my present Testament, I make and ordain mine executors, that is to say, John Ingilby, Prior of the Charter House of Shene, William Sutton, and Thomas Brent, Doctors; and I beseech my said dearest daughter; the Queen's grace, and my son Thomas, Marquess of Dorset, to put their good wills, and help for the performance of this my Testament.

In witness whereof, to this my present Testament, I have set my seal; these witnesses, John, Abbot of Saint Saviour of Bermondsey, and Benedictus Cum, Doctor of Physic. Given the year and day aforesaid [Nicholas 7].

This last will of England's once lovely queen surely touched even the coldest of hearts, save that of the husband of her own daughter!

Queen Elizabeth's eldest son, Thomas, Lord Grey of Groby, was created Earl of Huntingdon by his father-in-law in 1471. He soon resigned the title and was created Marquess of Dorset and Knight of the Garter on April 18, 1475. Soon after the death of Edward IV, his relationship with the young king came under suspicion. He was attained of high treason in the first year of Richard III's reign, though he was fully restored when Henry VII ascended the throne in 1485. When he died in 1501, his son Thomas succeeded him as second Marquess of Dorset. Thomas, a celebrated soldier, distinguished himself in jousts and tournaments. He was also elected a Knight of the Garter. When Thomas died in 1530, his son and heir Henry Grey inherited all his father's honors — the Marquisate of Dorset and the Baronies of Ferrers of Groby, Astley, Bonville and Harington. The last two he garnered from the marriage of Thomas, the first Marquess, to Cecily Bonville, who inherited Harington from her father and Bonville from her great-grandfather.

On October 11, 1551, Edward VI raised the Marquess of Dorset to the Dukedom of Suffolk, a dignity which had become extinct that year on the death without issue of the Marchioness' half-brother Henry Brandon, Duke of Suffolk; on the same day, John Dudley, Earl of Warwick, was created Duke of Northumberland.

Lady Jane Grey, the eldest daughter of Henry Grey and the Lady Frances Brandon, is reckoned to have been born in October 1537, at Bradgate in Leicestershire. History has recorded nothing of her early years.

It is safe to speculate that Jane Grey's education was carefully supervised. Though her eulogists describe her as well versed in Latin, Greek, Hebrew, Chaldaic, Arabic, French and Italian, such learning was neither customary nor useful in the education of a female of the time. Indeed, a whole lifetime would be scarcely sufficient to attain half the proficiency in seven languages some writers ascribe to her. Those same writers also indicate proficiency in playing musical instruments and at needlework, though no contemporary documents support their claims. More likely, Lady Jane's tutors may have provided slight exposure to some or all those languages, but to assume her proficiency extended beyond Greek, Latin, and French would be questionable.

It has been suggested that her principal tutor was John Aylmer, afterward Bishop of London. Early biographies attribute part of her achievements to Roger Ascham. In 1551, prior to his departure for Germany, Ascham visited her at Bradgate and his account of the interview affords interesting information about her pursuits and disposition. His well-known account was included in the opening scenes of a popular movie about Lady Jane. Ascham reports that, upon arrival, he found the Marquess and Marchioness of Dorset hunting in the park with their attendants, while Lady Jane was in her chamber reading the *Phaedo* of Plato in Greek; to his inquiry why she did not join in the family amusement, she replied with a smile,

"I wisse [think] all their sport in the park is but a shadow to that pleasure that I find in Plato. Alas, good folk, they never felt what true pleasure means."

Ascham then asked: "And how came you, madam, to this deep knowledge of pleasure, and what did chiefly allure you unto it, seeing not many women, but very few men have attained thereunto?"

"I will tell you," she replied, "and tell you a truth, which perchance you will marvel at. One of the greatest benefits that ever God gave me, is that he sent me so sharp and severe parents, and so gentle a schoolmaster, for when I am in presence either of father or mother, whether I speak, keep silence, sit, stand, or go, eat, drink, be merry, or sad, be sewing, playing, dancing, or doing anything else, I must do it as it were in such weight, measure, and number, even so perfectly as God made the world; or else I am so sharply taunted, so cruelly threatened, yea, presently sometimes with pinches, nips, bobs, and other ways which I will not name for the honour I bear them; so without measure disordered, that I think myself in hell till the time come that I must go to Mr. Elmer, who teacheth me so gently, so pleasantly, with such fair allurements to learning, that I think all the time nothing, whilst I am with him; and when I am called from him I fall on weeping, because whatsoever I do else but learning is full of great trouble, fear, and whole misliking unto me; and thus my book hath been so much my pleasure, and bringeth daily to me more pleasure, and more that in respect of it all other pleasures in very deed be but trifles and troubles unto me [Nicholas 10-11].

Lady Jane's religious accomplishments were in part the legacy of her tutors. The best known of them, though she wrote only three letters to him, was Zwingli's disciple and successor Henry Bullinger. Born July 18, 1504, in Bremgarten, a small town about ten miles west of Zurich, he evinced fondness for learning, application, and forwardness while young and made rapid advances in Latin studies and later in Hebrew and Greek literature.

On Sunday, June 21, 1528, he preached his first sermon in the village of Husen near Cappel. On December 9, 1531, he accepted the position of pastor in Zurich, in which important post he continued for the remainder of his long life. Though he survived the plague of

1541, he eventually succumbed to disease. A bright example of Christian patience, he died September 17, 1575.

Henry Bullinger's literary remains are extensive. A review of his contributions leaves little wonder why Lady Jane regarded him so highly. Lady Jane wrote him three letters between July 1551 and June 1553. They are among the very few documents by Lady Jane's own hand still in existence. The original letters are currently housed in the Zurich Library.

Letter 1 was dated at Bradgate, July 12, 1551, when Lady Jane was just thirteen years old. It was sent to Zurich enclosed in one from John ab Ulmis bearing the same date.

I give you, most learned sir, unceasing thanks, and shall do so as long as I live, for I cannot engage to requite the obligation; as I seem to myself quite unable to make a suitable return for such exceeding courtesy, unless indeed you should be of the opinion that I return a favor while I retain it in my remembrance. Nor are these professions made without reason. For I have received from you a most weighty and eloquent epistle, which was indeed very gratifying to me, not only because, to the neglect of more important engagements, you have condescended to write from so distant a country, and in your declining age, to me, who am unworthy of the correspondence of so distinguished a personage; but also because your writings are of such a character, as that they contain, not mere ordinary topics for amusement, but pious and divine thoughts for instruction, admonition and counsel, on such points especially, as are suited to my age and sex and the dignity of my family. In this epistle, as in every thing else that you have published to the great edification of the Christian commonwealth, you have shewn yourself not only a man of exquisite learning and singular acquirement, but also a skillful, prudent, and godly counsellor; one who can relish nothing that is not excellent, think nothing that is not divine, enjoin nothing that is not profitable, and produce nothing that is not virtuous, pious, and worthy of so reverend a father. Oh! happy me, to be possessed of such a friend and so wise a counsellor! (for, as Solomon says, "in the multitude of counsellors there is safety") and to be connected by the ties of friendship and intimacy with so learned a man, so pious a divine, and so intrepid a champion of true religion! On many accounts I consider myself beholden to Almighty God; but especially for having, after I was bereaved of the pious Bucer, that most learned man and holy father, who unweariedly did not cease, day and night, and to the utmost of his ability, to supply me with all necessary instructions and directions for my conduct in life; and who by his excellent advice promoted and encouraged my progress and advancement in all virtue, godliness, and learning; for having, I say, afforded me in his place a man so worthy to be reverenced as yourself, and who, I hope, will continue, as you have begun, to spur me on, when I loiter and am inclined to delay. For no better fortune can wait me than to be thought worthy of the correspondence and most wholesome admonitions of men so renowned, whose virtues cannot be sufficiently eulogized; and to experience the same happiness as was enjoyed by Blesilla, Paula, and Eustochium, to whom, as it is recorded, Saint Jerome imparted instruction, and brought them by his discourses to the knowledge of divine truths; or, the happiness of that venerable matron, to whom St. John addressed an exhortatory and evangelical epistle; or that, lastly, of the mother of Severus, who profited by the counsels of Origen, and was obedient to his precepts. All which personages were less indebted for their renown and celebrity to their beauty of person, nobility of birth, and large possessions, than to the glory and happiness they derived from the instructions of wise men, who, though singularly eminent for erudition and piety, did not disdain to lead them, as it were, by the hand to every thing excellent, and to suggest to them such thoughts as might especially conduce to their eternal salvation and happiness in the life to come. And I request again and again, that as you cannot be deemed inferior to any of these in understanding, or learning, or godliness, you will condescend to manifest a like kindness to myself. My unreserved requests may carry with them an appearance of boldness; but if you will consider the motive by which I am actuated, namely, that I may draw forth from the storehouse of your piety such instruction as may tend both to direct my conduct, and confirm my faith in Christ my Saviour, your goodness cannot, and your wisdom will not, allow you to censure them.

From that little volume of pure and unsophisticated religion, which you lately sent to my father and myself, I gather daily, as out of a most beautiful garden, the sweetest flowers. My father also, as far as his weighty engagements permit, is diligently occupied in the perusal of it: but whatever advantage either of us may derive from thence, we are bound to render thanks to you for it, and to God on your account; for we cannot think it right to receive with ungrateful minds such and so many truly divine benefits, conferred by Almighty God through the instrumentality of yourself and those like you, not a few of whom Germany is now in this respect so happy as to possess. If it be customary with mankind, as indeed it ought to be, to return favor for favor, and to shew ourselves mindful of benefits bestowed; how much rather should we endeavor to embrace with joyfulness the benefits conferred by divine goodness, and at least to acknowledge them with our gratitude, though we may be unable to make an adequate return!

I now come to that part of your letter which contains a commendation of myself, which as I cannot claim, so also I ought not to allow: but whatever the divine goodness may have bestowed upon me, I ascribe solely to himself, as the chief and sole author of any thing in me that bears any semblance of what is good; and to whom I entreat you, most accomplished sir, to offer your constant prayers on my behalf, that he may so direct me and all my actions, that I may not be found unworthy of his so great goodness. My most noble father would have written to you, to thank you both for the important labors in which you are engaged, also for the singular courtesy you have manifested by inscribing with his name and publishing under his auspices your fifth Decade, had he not been summoned by most weighty business in his majesty's service to the remotest parts of Britain; but as soon as public affairs shall afford him leisure, he is determined, he says, to write you with all diligence. To conclude, as I am now beginning to learn Hebrew, if you will point out some way and method of pursuing this study to the greatest advantage, you will confer on me a very great obligation.

Farewell, brightest ornament and support of the whole church of Christ; and may Almighty God long preserve you to us and to his church!

Your most devoted,

Jane Grey.

Letter 2 was dated at Bradgate, July 7, 1552.

I should seem altogether ungrateful, unmindful of my duty, and unworthy of your favors, could I do otherwise than thank you, most accomplished sir, for your many acts of kindness to myself. I do this however with diffidence, inasmuch as the great friendship which you desire to exist between us, and the many favors you have conferred upon one who is so entirely undeserving of them, seem to demand something more than mere thanks; and I cannot satisfactorily repay by my poor and worthless correspondence the debt of gratitude I owe you. The consideration also of my unfit-ness to address a letter to a person of your eminence, greatly adds to my uncomfortable feelings; nor indeed should I either desire or presume to disturb your important labors with my trifles and puerilities, or interrupt your eloquence by my so great rudeness of speech, only that I know I have no other means of testifying my gratitude, and that I have no doubt of your accustomed and long experienced indulgence.

With respect to the letter I lately received from you, you must know, that after having read it twice over, (for one perusal did not satisfy me,) I seemed to have derived as much benefit from your excellent and truly divine precepts, as I have scarcely obtained from the daily perusal of the best authors. You exhort me to embrace a genuine and sincere faith in Christ my Saviour. I will endeavor to satisfy you in this respect, as far as God shall enable me to do; but as I acknowledge faith to be his gift, I ought there-fore only to promise so far as he may see fit to bestow it upon me. I shall not however cease to pray, with the apostils, that he may of his goodness daily increase it in me. And to this I will add, as you exhort me, and with the divine blessing, such holiness of life, as my (alas!) too feeble powers may enable me to practice. Do you, meanwhile, with your wonted kindness, make daily mention of me in your prayers. In the study of Hebrew I shall pursue that method which you so clearly point out. Farewell, and may God protect you in the task you have undertaken, and prosper you for evermore!

Your most religiously obedient,
Jane Grey.

Letter 3 was dated before June 1553.

The tardy performance of a duty, most learned sir, ought not to be censured, especially if it has not been omitted through neglect. The truth is, I am at a great distance from you, the couriers are few, and news reaches me slowly: but as I can now avail myself of the messenger, by whom my letters to you, and yours to me, have usually been conveyed, I must not be wanting in my duty of writing to you, but as diligently as possible, by word and deed, discharge the obligation. For so great is your authority with all men, so great, as I hear, is the solidity of your preaching, so great too is the integrity of your conduct, according to the report of those who know you, that foreign and remote nations, as well as your own countrymen, are excited not only by your words, but by your actions, to follow after a good and happy life. For you are not only, as St James says, a diligent herald and preacher of the gospel, and of the holy commands of God, but also a true observer and doer of them; and you manifest in your own life the practice that your precepts enjoin, not deceiving yourself. Neither, indeed, do you resemble those who behold their natural face in a glass, and, as soon as they have gone away, forget the form of it; but you preach true and sound doctrine, and by your manner of life afford an example and pattern for others to follow what you both enjoin and practice. But why so I thus address you gravely, when my ignorance is such that I can neither adequately praise your piety, nor sufficiently eulogise your integrity of life, nor set forth your profound and admirable learning in a becoming manner? Were I indeed to extol you as truth requires, I should need either the oratorical powers of Demosthenes, or the eloquence of Cicero; for your merits are so great, as to demand not only length of time, but an acuteness of intellect and elegance of expression far beyond that of my age to set them forth. For God, it seems, has looked upon you with such complacency, as to have fitted you both for his kingdom and for this world: for in this earthly prison you pass your days, as though you were dead; whereas you live, and this not only to Christ in the first place, without whom there can be no life, and in the next place to yourself; but also to others without number, whom you strenuously labor and assiduously endeavor to bring, by God's blessing, to that immortality which, when you shall have departed this life, you will obtain yourself. And that your piety may accomplish what you desire, I will not cease to implore of God, the supreme ruler of the universe, nor constantly to importune the divine ears for your long continuance in this life.

In writing to you in this manner I have exhibited more bold-ness than prudence: but so great has been your kindness towards me, in condescending to write to me, a stranger, and in supplying the necessary instruction for the adornment of my understanding and the improvement of my mind, that I should justly appear chargeable with neglect and forgetfulness of duty, were [I] not to shew myself mindful of you and of your deservings in every possi-ble way. Besides, I entertain the hope that you will excuse the more than feminine boldness of me, who, girlish and unlearned as I am, presume to write a man who is the father of learning; and that you will pardon that rudeness which has made me not hesitate to interrupt your more important occupations with my vain trifles and puerile correspondence. Let me but obtain your indulgence, and I shall consider myself on every account exceedingly indebted to your kindness. For if I have been to blame in this matter, you must ascribe it rather to the excess of my regard for you and for your virtues, than either to a boldness which ought not at all to exist in our sex, or a temerity which is for the most part adverse to our better judgment; inasmuch as the splendor of your endow-ments is so dazzling to my mental perception, whenever I read your works or meditate upon yourself, that I do not consider what is becoming to my condition, but what is due to your worth and excellence. My mind, moreover, is fluctuating and undecided: for while I consider my age, sex, and mediocrity, or rather infancy of learning, each of these things, much more all of them, deter me from writing; but when I call to mind the eminence of your vir-tues, the celebrity of your character, and the magnitude of your favors towards me, the higher consideration yields to the inferior; a sense of what is becoming me gives way to your worth, and the respect which your merits demand usually prevails over all other considerations.

It now only remains for me, most illustrious sir, earnestly to entreat you cordially to salute in my name, though I am personally unacquainted with him, the excellent Bibliander, that pattern of erudition, godliness, and authority. For so great is the reputation of his learning in our country, and so renowned his name among all people, by reason of the singular endowments which God has bestowed upon him, that though I have acquired but little learn-ing myself, I cannot resist my inclination to pay respect to the piety and integrity of such a man, who, if I am not mistaken, has been sent to us from heaven. And I pray God that such pillars of the church as you both are, may long enjoy good health. As long as I shall be permitted to live, I shall not cease to offer you my good wishes, to thank you for the kindness you have shewed me, and to pray for your welfare. Farewell, learned sir.

Your piety's most devoted,

Jane Grey[Harding 4].

Arguably, John Dudley, the Duke of Northumberland, was the key player in determining Lady Jane's fate, and it seems appropriate to include a brief biography of him here. Very little is known about John Dudley's early years. Nothing set him apart from others of his social level. John was born probably in 1504. The act of Parliament that restored him in blood in 1512 described him as under eight years of age (Beer 7).

The eldest of Edmund's sons, John received an appointment to a lieutenancy in the army in 1523. Serving under the Duke of Suffolk, he campaigned in France and was knighted with Edward Seymour.

He later served King Henry VIII at court and in the country and became an established figure. His military reputation was by far his greatest achievement and guaranteed respect — until his downfall in the summer of 1553, as this unfolding story will reveal. In 1537 (the year Lady Jane was born), John Dudley was appointed vice-admiral of a small fleet to combat the Flemish. This success earned him the title of "Lord of the Channel Seas" (Beer 9).

His political achievements were many. He entered Parliament in 1534, succeeding Sir Edward Guildford of Kent. Dudley realized early on that a position of office could be profitable and was certainly the avenue to a higher social level and political power in Tudor England. It was those ambitions that eventually led to his downfall almost twenty years later.

Edward VI, also a key figure in Lady Jane's fate, showed none of the selfish intent of the Duke of Northumberland.

Jane Seymour's pregnancy by Henry VIII, announced on May 27, 1537, produced a boy, Edward, on October 12, 1537. On October

15, he was baptized and proclaimed Duke of Cornwall. Edward grew up in the splendor one would expect. His education began early, and he was regarded as a fast learner. His education included literature, geography, and music. Like his father, Edward played the lute and possibly other instruments.

After his father's death on January 28, 1547, Edward (at the age of nine) became more involved in court, and as the young king grew older, the festivities grew more elaborate and expensive.

Edward enjoyed a wide range of physical activities and sports, such as archery and hunting. He was very much his father's son, interested in warfare. He enjoyed watching tournaments and jousts and participated in them.

In early February 1553, at the age of fifteen, the king came down with a feverish cold. He did not recover, as he had from others in the past, and on March 1 he was forced to open a new session of Parliament in the great chamber of Whitehall instead of going to Westminster. The young king was unable to go to Greenwich for Easter as he had hoped, "still troubled with catarrh and a cough" (Loach, 159).

News of Edward's illness, more severe than his past ailments, spread quickly through the kingdom. Many, including his own physicians, feared that the Lord would take him from them soon. The once vibrant and active king was confined to his bed and grew weaker with each passing day.

In the second week of April, Edward felt well enough to move to Greenwich and though he remained weak, he made a public appearance in the gardens the day after he arrived.

The Duke of Northumberland, realizing the young king had little time left, began to conceive a plan which is revealed in a letter from him to the Duke of Suffolk, written in late April or early May of 1553.

My Lord Duke,
The increasing ill-symptoms of the King's disorder, cannot but alarm all who love their country; nor can I think of that ignorant

bigot, Mary, succeeding to the crown, without horror: the thought has always given the King great uneasiness.

I have been thinking of an expedient, nor can I banish it from my thoughts; and have at length formed a plan, which I want your, and the Duchess of Suffolk's concurrence in, before I can proceed to communicate it to the King.

You know that his father, King Henry, thought proper to set aside the succession of his daughters, Mary and Elizabeth, to the crown of England, after their brother Edward, by pronouncing them illegitimate; though indeed he afterwards restored their claims again.

However, Mary's religion is a sufficient reason for setting aside her claim, and Elizabeth cannot be appointed to the exclusion of her sister. The next in succession is Mary, Princess of Scotland, but being a foreigner, she is naturally excluded; then claims your Duchess in right of her mother, who was niece to Henry.

What I wish your concurrence in, is, to persuade the Duchess to accept the crown, should Edward be prevailed on to appoint her his successor; or in case of her refusal, to urge her daughter, Lady Jane, to accept it. This, my lord, if you can accomplish, we will endeavor to prevail on Edward to make such a destination, and get the patent ready for him to sign immediately.

I am aware that it is not without a prospect of difficulty, that this plan can be executed; but the love of religion and my country, will enable me to undertake the most arduous pursuits, to procure the happiness of the one, and the firm establishment of the other.

I have no doubt, but the other party will impute this scheme to my ambitious views for my son; but I should be wholly unfit for my rank in life, and unworthy [of] the spirit of my ancestors, should I stoop to regard what the people say of me.

Let me prevail on you to follow my example, my dear friend, in this respect; let us think and act nobly, and independently of the clamors and applauses of the multitude, and pursue what is for the public good without mean and vulgar considerations. Your Duchess, or Lady Jane, would adorn the throne, and the King, you know, is highly attached to both, and has the most tender and brotherly affection for your excellent daughter.

Let me hope that you will exert your influence over them in this affair, and that you see things in a proper point of view.

I am, My Lord Duke,

Your devoted Friend, Northumberland [Lane 80].

Northumberland reveals only a portion of his plan as he appeals to the Duke of Suffolk to consider the fate of the kingdom, should Edward die.

Indirectly, the letter reveals that besides placing Lady Jane on the throne, Northumberland wanted to marry his only unwed son, Guildford, to her and make his son a king. With his son as king, Northumberland could consolidate his grip on power and status.

The surprised and slightly perplexed Duke of Suffolk received the letter with caution and suspicion, as shown in his reply to Northumberland:

> My Lord Protector,
> The contents of your Grace's letter filled my mind with a variety of different reflections, which have perplexed and agitated it greatly.
> I doubtless regret, as do all the friends of the reformation, the consequences of the King's approaching dissolution. Yet have I never entertained a thought, that the Princess Mary's claim to the succession could be set aside; much less that it can be possible, or just, to exclude every prior claim, in favor of the Duchess of Suffolk's.
> You have conducted me into a labyrinth, the clue of which I can not unravel. You, who know the excellencies of my daughter, and the ardency of my affection for her, will readily imagine, how delightful is the idea of seeing her on the Throne of England, whose glory and happiness she would prove. But I check this visionary prospect, from the still stronger feelings of justice and equity.
> Thence am I recalled to the ideal view of Mary, placed on that Throne, and fraught with superstition, dealing around her tyranny and persecution. The miseries of an oppressed people! The reformation, which cost her father so much difficulty to establish, destroyed in blood! and liberty, the parent of every virtue, and of every comfort, to a nation for ever crushed!
> My mind then reverts to the origin of government. Was it the selection of a person to be King, who was to possess an unbounded license to tyrannize over the persons, properties, lives, and even opinions of their subjects? — Or, was it the selection of a person, whose virtues had gained him the preference to his equals,

and whom they had appointed, in consequence of this preference, to be their Father, their Protector, and their King?

What a blessing does such a King prove to a nation! — Under his reign smiles [*sic*], commerce flourishes, vice is discountenanced, and religion pure, simple, and unincumbered with needless ceremonies, proceeds from the heart, and actuates the manner of his people.

Let this amiable Prince resign his life into the hands of his Maker; would the heir of such a King, in the first ages, known to be of a disposition tyrannical and oppressive, having no rule of conduct but his own selfish and unrestrained will, nor any pursuit but to shew his authority by cruelty; would such a one be next appointed to reign, and this tyranny be considered as an hereditary and undoubted right, through all succeeding generations? would the Councellors of such a King recommend him as his successor? Would they not rather consider it an injustice to do it, since so many thousands would be the miserable sufferers?

These considerations have their weight with me, in relation to your proposal of setting Mary aside; but not entirely in favor of my daughter, since the Princess Elizabeth is a worthy Lady, and a Protestant.

Greatly as I concur with you in my desires, I would not pursue them against the conviction of my conscience. You must, therefore, my Lord, produce some prevailing argument, to enable me to give my acquiescence to your proposal. Was my mind perfectly convinced of the justice of my cause, I would not regard the clamors or applauses of the people, but steadily pursue my purpose; but I cannot act in contradiction to what I esteem beyond every thing, the principles of justice, and the acquiescence of conscience. I may be mistaken in my present views of the affair, but will see your Grace this evening, or to-morrow; we will then converse on it more freely, and if you can convince me you [are] right, I will use every means in my power to promote so agreeable a scheme.

I mentioned it to the Duchess, who has far less objection to it than I have, but who would resign her claim to her daughter.

Yet from Lady Jane, I think, we should find some difficulty. She has a passion for retirement, and no ambition to prompt her wish for a Crown.

The happiness of this charming daughter, and your worthy son, is the delight of her mother and myself; nor can it, I think, obtain an addition from any thing the world can procure them.

19

Most happy would it render me, did it please the Almighty to spare the King's life a little longer, who has a Throne in the hearts of his subjects, and who is dear to me as a son; but I fear our hopes are vain for so great a blessing.
I remain, my Lord Duke,
Your Grace's, &c.
Suffolk [Lane 86].

Clearly, the Duke of Suffolk was uncomfortable with Northumberland's plan, but they shared the same opinion and concern about the kingdom, should Mary succeed Edward.

Northumberland managed to persuade the Duke of Suffolk to support his ideas and soon began discussing a change in the order of succession with Edward, who was at first not willing to change his father's will. The Duke's plan was based in part on the little known fact that Parliament had already declared the marriages of Henry VIII to Katherine of Aragon and Anne Boleyn illegitimate, thus making their daughters, the Lady Mary and the Lady Elizabeth, bastards, and invalidating their claim to the crown.

The Duke believed that if Mary succeeded, she would impose popery on the nation, thus undoing all her father had achieved and Edward had striven for. To persuade the King, the Duke reasoned that if Mary or Elizabeth succeeded, "she might marry a stranger, and the laws and liberties of England would be sacrificed and the religion changed" (Chapman, *Lady Jane Grey*, 89).

Edward finally agreed to remove Mary from the order of succession but then questioned the removal of Elizabeth's rights; though younger, she was of the reformed religion. Northumberland quickly responded. "The Lady Mary could not be put by unless the Lady Elizabeth were put by also, as their rights depended upon one another" (*ibid.*).

The Duke emphasized that the King should set the affairs of his kingdom in order to insure that his wishes would be carried out after his death. "It becomes the part of a religious and good prince to set apart all respects of blood where God's glory and the subjects' weal may be endangered. That your Majesty should do otherwise

20

were, after this short life, to expect revenge at God's dreadful tribunal" (*ibid.*).

After further persuasion by Northumberland, the King finally agreed to remove his half sisters from the order of succession. Next, Mary Queen of Scots was removed on the grounds that in devoting herself to Scottish affairs she had forfeited her English rights. Next was Frances Brandon, now the Duchess of Suffolk (Jane's mother), who declined because of her age; at least, this was the official reason given. Quite probably, other influences persuaded her to decline. Finally, they arrived at Lady Jane Grey. Edward was pleased and comfortable to leave his kingdom to her for many reasons, and so he set the Duke of Northumberland's plan in motion.

In *The Chronicle of Queen Jane*, John G. Nichols points out the change in wording in Edward's devise: "The next alternative was to appoint the Lady Jane to be the positive heir to the throne. This was actually done by altering the words in his will from "....to the L' Jane's heires masles" to "...to the L' Jane and her heires masles."

Nichols further indicates that in the King's devise, a pen line is drawn through the letter "s", which still remains on the paper, and the words "and her" are written above the line.

The Duke of Northumberland's confidence was high, since he had successfully manipulated Edward to change his father's will. With the devise in rough draft, his son was even closer to marrying the putative queen.

At the end of the first week or the beginning of the second week of May, Jane wrote a letter to her cousin, Lady Anne Grey. Now aged fifteen, Jane was unaware of any marriage plans and gave no hint of them. Curiously, in the seventh paragraph Jane mentions the "the bare possibility of being queen," indicating that she was aware of the original order of succession Henry VIII had laid out, but not of the recent changes.

> How painful, my dearest friend and cousin, is this our first sep-
> aration! — in vain does nature, in the delightful dress of May,
> present her opening charms to my senses, and endeavor to com-

pose and exhilarate my soul, by the cheerful woodland song — the floweret's blooming tints and refreshing fragrance — the gilded Aurora, or serene Hesperus — the voice of the cheerful shepherd carols in vain — in vain the more polished notes of refined music — or the enchanting beauties of Grecian poetry solicit my attention — the whole of the harmonious feast is tasteless, while unparticipated with the friend of my heart.

You are about to be presented to that Court which I have never yet seen, and feel, I know not why, a shivering at my heart whenever I but think of seeing it.

That series of history, which we have read together, how frequently has it inspired us with disgust of Courts and Royalty.

We know not the world by our own experience, but history affords us the experience of ages; and, alas, where have we found Princes better or happier than the meanest and most obscure peasant?

How weighty their cares? how embittered their pleasures? how insecure their greatness!

What would I give, my cousin, had I been born in a more humble station. The bare possibility of being a Queen, is a source of uneasiness to me, though it is very improbable I shall ever be one.

But your lively disposition may, perhaps, be dazzled with the charms and pleasures of the Court; and you may no longer relish those simple, but rational amusements, which we enjoyed together, and which, without you, are become uninteresting to me.

Is it not probable, also, that the noble youths of England will flock around my fair cousin, and solicit that heart which I have prized as my own treasure?

But then, how divided will be your affections, and how greatly will the torch of love obscure and eclipse the lamp of friendship? — Ah! that it may not wholly extinguish it!

What a cruel distance also may, perhaps, divide us! — You must accompany a husband, while I, who never wish to know the magic influence of love, shall be left to prove it in solitude, that nothing in life is desirable without the friend — the sister of my heart.

Ah! my Anne, hasten from the insidious Court, to the once delightful shades of S-. Hasten to your Jane — speedily come, and impart to her all you have seen, and all you have felt, nor let my

heart pine for your absence. My letters will remind you of me —
let me not expect, in vain, the speedy return of your's.

Farewell,

Jane Grey [Lane 7].

In the second week of May, Jane wrote in a letter to Lady Anne
that "they" have been talking to her of marriage and of Guildford
Dudley for the first time. "They" perhaps were her parents, who had
discussed the subject of marriage with her before, perhaps when she
was only eleven years old; but now, obviously, the motivation had
changed.

In the last paragraph of the letter, Jane refers to the "once
delightful shades of S-", possibly a reference to their residence at
Syon.

I am a little recovered from those first emotions which our separation excited — and have been indulging this reflection, that we
should not live to ourselves, because society has claims on our
exertions for its happiness.

That though our exalted station enables us to choose our
employments, it brings with it obligations to public usefulness,
which those are not under, whose necessities compel them to
attend on their daily labor. And that our talents, however common
they may be, yet when drawn out, and cultivated by a superior
education, have far higher ends than merely to amuse us, or flatter
our supercilious pride. Viewed only in this light, they become con-
temptible, and often render women, of an excentric education,
objects of ridicule.

Such women are too apt to neglect the proper duties of the sex
and character, and become solicitous to be admired for a few useless accomplishments, which they would be much more amiable
without.

When my father chose to give me some ideas of philosophy,
and the learned languages, and prevailed on your's, that we should
be educated together, with our cousin the Royal Edward, you cannot but remember how studious they were to inculcate these sentiments upon our minds; and to inspire us with humility, at the
same time that the fields of science were opening before us.

Delightful instructors! — What most interesting and pleasing
truths did you gradually unfold to us, as our ripening judgments

could receive them? — What noble discoveries did you make to our astonished faculties, in the wonders of natural philosophy, and, above all things, the greater wonders of revealed truth? — What gratitude! What humanity! What hopes! What delight have we felt in our glowing bosoms, as we attended with fixed attention, to our revered tutor? — And as we listened to his gentle precepts, for the conduct of our lives, how have our meeting eyes read the feelings of each other's heart! while the falling tear has tacitly imparted to our delighted preceptor, the impression which his lessons made on our tender minds?

O ye delightful days and years of peaceful instruction; enlivened with many a cheerful song and animated dance; with many a social ride and walk, as well as many a rural sport, which our superior birth prevented us not from sharing with the neighboring gentry. Shall we ever again engage in those pursuits; taste those pleasures together? — Why cannot I be permitted to continue the enjoyment of such a life, under the protection of my noble father? — Alas! why, young as I am, must my tender parents be thinking of parting with me?

Already, my Anne, have they been talking to me of marriage; informing me of the names of lovers who have seen and sought me; but only hinting at the rest, leaving it to time to expatiate on the merits of Lord Guildford Dudley, and of the advantageous alliance it will be for me.

Lord Guildford I have never seen, nor have I ever yet seen any man, who has for a moment engaged my attention as a lover. I have admired sense and merit where-ever I have found it, in the circle of my acquaintance, as far as my weak judgment would allow me to discriminate, but the name of love has ever been dreaded by me.

Surely my father will not urge me to marry, while a stranger to the passion; and at present I think I shall never experience it. My honored parents, my sister, and you, my Anne, fill up the inmost recesses of my heart; yet it is not so much engrossed, as not to leave ample room for philanthropy; and, indeed, I should hate myself could I, who am placed in so favored a lot, exclude the distrest from my compassion, or the indigent from my assistance.

The best wishes of thy Jane attend thee, my Anne.

Farewell [Lane 14].

Another letter to Lady Anne, written only two days later, indicates the further pressure on Jane from her parents. Responding to all the talk about the marriage to Guildford, she indicates she has "a dread of seeing him" and a "dislike" for the Dudley family.

I find you are universally admired, my dear cousin, and surrounded by a train of flattering lovers whenever you appear in public. — This I was informed of by a gentleman, who is lately arrived from court.

You say, only, that the novelty pleases you at present; but that you daily reflect on all you have heard and read of the Sirens of that enchanted circle, and distrust yourself. Dear admirable girl, may thy sweet humility, thy lively mirth, and tranquil heart, be never exchanged for haughty airs, obsequious flattery, wild ambition, and designing artifice, which rob the mind of its tranquility, and the cheek of its blossom.

Be not forgetful of your religious duties, my cousin; the vivacity of your disposition exposes you to many snares, which we have been told are laid in the great world, for the credulous and unwary.

How shall I rejoice at your return? I fear I shall not find you the same unaffected friend I once knew you: but away with those fears: is not your heart the feat of innocence and virtue? has it not been early sown with every principle of sacred piety, with the feeds of every moral duty? has it not been early taught to scorn all meanness, all insincerity? though so young, is not your judgment mature? Let me not then distrust either the head or heart of my friend, but commit her to the protection of that Providence, whose care has hitherto defended her.

My mind is not so cheerful as it used to be. — I earnestly wish for your presence. — I want to communicate a thousand things to you, which I cannot write. — This Lord Guildford — a dread of seeing him — a fear of offending my much-loved parents, by not being able to approve of him; a disinclination to be married so young: all those reflections continually agitate my mind with a painful solicitude. Besides all this, I dislike the family of Lord Guildford. His father, the Duke of Northumberland's ambition, is but too well known to our house; and the indignities Lord Somerset suffered from him, who was at last the principle cause of his untimely fate. — In alliance with that haughty and artful nobleman I foresee a thousand evils.

Adieu, hasten to your

Jane Grey [Lane 22].

The next letter is the first reply letter we have from Lady Anne to Lady Jane. Anne appears to be preoccupied with her own futile affection for the king, and not with Lady Jane's affliction. She hints at the time at which her letter was written in the antepenultimate paragraph, with "The advance of summer," which could place the letter in the second or third week of May.

I have at last been presented to the Royal Edward, and was graciously received; but if I always loved and admired him as one child loves another, in our happy infantile days, how was I dazzled with admiration, when I beheld his youthful and elegant form; his lucid eyes softened with the mild beams of sweet benevolence; that air of dignity, softened by affability, which discovers superior worth and talents. — I cannot find language to express my feelings.

I knelt down, and was intending respectfully to kiss his hand, but he hastily took mine. — No, it must not be, my dear Lady Anne, the companion of my happy hours of childhood, when I was a stranger to the forms and restraints of royalty. — He saluted me, and continued — It is with extreme pleasure that I see you, and any of the Duke of Suffolk's family; you will honor my court with your presence sometime, I hope.

I felt myself very much embarrassed, but answered him as cheerfully and freely as I could. I have since frequently injoined friendly conversations with him, in company with my father, or Lady Dudley, when he has treated me like a sister; has been as playful in wit, as full of entertaining vivacity, as he used to be when a boy; though highly improved by ripened understanding, the accomplishments of education, and the polish of a court.

But shall I tell you a secret? I find those interviews dangerous; there are none in Edward's court like their monarch: and though I have many admirers, I can listen to none of them; he alone is the sovereign of my soul. — But I have no hope; Edward has been too much accustomed to consider me as his sister, to think of me in any other light: besides, Edward is a king; he must seek an alliance with some foreign Princess, and it is imagined that he still retains an attachment to the beautiful Mary of Scotland.

I am convinced there is no hope, and, if it was in my power, I would fly from his presence before my heart is too far entangled; but I am obliged to remain here.

26

What would my father think, if I expressed a wish to leave him almost as soon as I arrived? Surely he would think, the Duke of Suffolk's family had engrossed all my affections, and annihilated the natural love which I owe my own.

No, I must stay here; but I will converse with the King as little as I possibly can.

Fear not, my dear Lady Jane, that your noble parents will force your inclinations in your choice of a husband. — I have often seen Lord Guildford Dudley at Lady Dudley's, where you may imagine your sister's company very frequently attracts me. — He is one of the handsomest, and most accomplished young noblemen about the court, and the most intimate bosom friend of his royal master: they are, indeed, congenial souls in taste and virtue.

Examples of vice, vanity, and trifling, are not wanting in Edward's court, though that from the throne is so bright a one: but be assured, my charming cousin, that I can be in no danger of imitating those follies and vices, while I have Edward's brightness before my face; for I can see nothing else, and detest every thing which he disapproves. I felt no less sensible than yourself, my separation from the friend of my heart: it was happy for me to meet Lady Catherine in town, as her company, in some measure, supplies your place.

We are now, as when with you, almost inseparable. Lady Dudley is perfectly friendly, and contributes all in her power to keep me in town, by her assiduity to find entertainment for me; but I shall gladly return to the happy shades of S-, as soon as my father will part with me.

The advance of summer renders London disagreeable, and I am tired of those amusements which novelty alone attracted my attention to. I am conscious of an unhappily placed affection, and the discipline and restraints which my reason impose on my thoughts and behaviour when with the King, render my situation here a painful one.

We were designed by our Creator unavoidably to suffer from our own unruly passions, the most virtuous of which unrestrained, would be a source of misery to us; but the lamp of reason was given us to illuminate our doubtful path, and conduct us back to wisdom: and when retirement shall again yield me more leisure for reflection, and absence lessen the impression I have received, I hope my dear Jane will still find in me her own.

Anne Grey [Lane 27].

The next letter Lady Jane wrote to her cousin reveals for the first time her growing awareness of her own awakening passions and of the confused emotions resulting from her introduction to Sir William Morley.

In my last letter I wrote you that a Gentleman from Court had given me an account of your Ladyship, of whom he spoke in the highest terms.

I was much pleased with his appearance and conversation — yet felt a confusion and restraint, when conversing with him, which abated my pleasure. He has been at my father's a fortnight, and is assiduous to ingratiate himself in my favor. Indeed, I have never been so much attached to the company of any man, except my father.

But that I may not be disingenuous to the friend, to whom I ought to reveal every sensation and folly of my heart, I will freely acknowledge a sentiment which lies on my conscience like guilt, and which I know not how to account for — but I really feel quite uneasy, when I hear the praises of my absent friend, from the lips of Sir William Morley. — Can it be envy? is it possible so baneful a passion could find admittance into the heart of your Jane?

I feel myself now less anxious for your return, and begin again to relish those parties of amusement, in which Sir William joins (in company with my parents) and in which he pays me the sole attention.

I sometimes begin to distrust my heart, and fear it is giving way, imperceptibly, to a growing passion for this agreeable stranger, and that what I have condemned in myself, as envy towards you, is the effect indeed of jealousy. But if it be so, however I might exculpate myself to the feelings of my Anne, I have not the less reason to dread the consequences to my own tranquility and future happiness, for this man has no distinguished honors, and, though of a respectable family, yet not of a noble one; consequently it will not, in my parents esteem, be a proper alliance for me; besides, he never entertained me on the subject of love. My birth demands from him the respect he pays me, more especially while under the roof of my father.

There is, however, in this Gentleman, a noble elevation of mind, such as would bespeak him of a high birth, were that and greatness of mind inseparable.

He displays a tender kind of esteem, in the attention he pays me, which is but too flattering to my heart; yet dispenses with that reserve from me, which I should be obliged to wear, should he have presumed to address me as a lover; yet his mind seems wholly superior to every mean art of insinuation, and too worthy and noble to seek the regard of others, by any thing but his intrinsic merit.

If you think my fears of a growing attachment to this man well-founded, forgive me, dear Lady Anne, my offence to you, though I can never forgive myself; for, though your Jane is subject to the weakness which accompany human passions, her heart, I hope, can never be so devoid of fortitude, so lost to friendship and filial love, as not to have the resolution to give up even a beloved object, if it interfered with the happiness of a friend or of parents.

I am struck with the similarity of our feelings at present, for I cannot deny to you, that I fear this man is making too deep an impression on my heart; and I find the thoughts of Lord Guildford more irksome to me than ever.

Hasten to me, my cousin, reassume your influence over my mind, and teach me to recover my former peaceful indifference.

Ever your's,
Jane Grey [Lane 36].

So, Jane admitted that Sir William made a favorable impression on her heart and that thought of Guildford still troubled her.

The next letter, also from Lady Jane to Anne, reflects events which have occurred to distinguish Jane's opinion of each man further. She is now convinced that she loves Sir William Morley, and her contempt for the Dudley family has grown.

How severe must the young lady's passion have been to make her say she has little pleasure in her studies, when Jane so prided herself on faithful diligence !

Sir William is obliged to go to town — he says he will endeavor to obtain permission to accompany the King (who I am exceedingly sorry to find is not well) in his journey through various parts of his kingdom, to which he is advised by his physicians.

He says he hopes his Majesty will pass some little time here, which he frequently talks of with pleasure.

"I may then," said he, "charming Lady Jane, have the happiness renewed, which I so infinitely prize, of enjoying once more your conversation, which none, who have experienced, can lose without reluctance."

The confusion with which he said this, and that with which I received it, could not, I think, but be visible to my parents. — He kissed my mother's hand and mine, and then hastily quitted us, and I retired to my apartment, at leisure to revolve in my thoughts the merit of this engaging youth, and to take my heart to task for being too sensible of it; I feel anew all the sensations of tasteless insipidity of being, which I first in my life felt at your leaving me.

I experience already but little pleasure in my studies, and the useful employments of my life. I am now perfectly convinced that I love him — I feel very little doubt, also, of his attachment to me — and yet, unless I can get the better of this prepossession in his favor, I see nothing, in my future life, that promises to fulfill the hopes which my parents have fondly conceived of me, or that can gratify their wishes, and permit me to render them happy by accepting the husband they have fixed on for me — Fixed on did I say! — Ah! how little do those know of the human heart, who imagine it is to be compelled to love.

Besides, it is not to gratify ambition, fatal ambition, that they want to unite me to the proud Northumberland's race?

Ah! my dear revered parents, this is your error. Not all my love and respect for you can prevent my discovering a feature in your character, which, I fear will conduct to misery.

What, my dear Lady Anne, but ambition can induce them so earnestly to wish an alliance with the Dudley's.

Did not Northumberland cause the attainder and death of my uncle, the Duke of Somerset, whose virtues were universally acknowledged and adored by the people?

Not all their misrepresentations of that bloody transaction, can prepossess my mind against him, not only as he was dear to me, but on account of Edward and his people, to whom he was in reality a protector. How can I regard, as I ought, the husband which they have designed for me, whose father was the murderer of my uncle?

Alas! poor Edward, how calamitous has been thy minority! and yet how much reason have we to dread still greater evils, from the ambition and vices of those around thee.

I entirely concur with you in opinion, my dear Lady Anne, that he is an ornament to the Throne, and, if it pleases the Almighty to spare his life, promises to be a blessing to England, and to complete the work his Royal Father began, and restore the holy Christian religion to its primitive purity. O how much reason have all to pray for his restored health, who love their country and the reformation? how much more reason have we to wish it, who know his worth and love his person?

Check your too great partiality for him, my cousin, and endeavor to confine it to friendship. He does love the fair Princess of Scotland, but in vain he loves her — his love is as fruitless as yours.

Prepare yourself, my dear, for whatever may happen, and should it please Heaven to take him from this world to a better, let us not lose that fortitude, which will enable us to support the loss, great as it will be.

Alas! my sad mind frequently anticipates something dreadful — his sister, the Princess Mary's obstinacy in the Romish faith. Her ignorance and bigotry gives him many an anxious reflection. England, indeed, has much to fear, should we lose the amiable Edward, from her inheriting the Crown. Her temper is the very reverse of his — and her faith allows, and even renders, persecution meritorious. Many a difficult task has his humanity had to combat with, in this age of fierce dispute on religious tenets; but, with the utmost reluctance, has he ever been persuaded to consent to severity.

But let us hope the best — one consolation tranquilizes my mind, when properly attended to, under every sinister event; which is, that an all-wise Providence superintends human affairs, and men can go no farther than they are permitted by him.

Adieu,

Jane Grey [Lane 43].

Lady Jane thus expresses more concern for the increasing possibility of Mary's accession, should Edward die, than for her star-crossed cousin's desire for a future with the King.

In Lady Anne's next letter to Jane, her father's interest in her marriage inhibits her hope to marry the King, and Lady Catherine, Jane's sister, also has a suitor.

My father has had application made to him of alliances in my behalf — but my heart rejects them all. You know that, peremptory as his temper is in general, yet his affection for me has always been of the gentlest and tenderest kind, nor would he oblige me to marry where I disapproved. He is, I must acknowledge ambitious, which, by the bye, is, I believe, a family feature, my Jane, though I have never found any thing of it in you; yet is he too fond of me not, on all occasions, to consult my happiness.

But he wants me to make a choice, and is very importunate with me to declare in favor of some of those who attach themselves to me — even the King urges me on the subject.

How irksome is their importunity! it is impossible, with a heart wholly devoted to that most excellent Prince, that I can fix on any other man — time alone can enable me to conquer my attachment to him — I fear I shall never do it, while I remain near him, and behold his transcendent merit.

I have a new affliction! — Edward is ill — his cough and complaints, which he had almost lost, are returned — his bloom is daily withering, and he seems like a fair rose blasted by too fervent a sun, just as its beauties were unfolding.

He was placed on the Throne too young. His ardent and mature mind could not be content to leave the affairs of state solely to the Protector, without more thought and anxious solicitude for the welfare of his people, than his youth could bear; the humane and compassionate turn of his disposition, surpass and crown his other virtues; and his beneficence to the poor, will perpetuate his name to posterity, for the many noble public charities established by him; while the graces and virtues of his private manners and conduct, endear him, beyond expression, to all who attend on him, or are blest with his more intimate friendship.

He is advised, as you have been informed, to visit some of the provinces of his kingdom, to assist the recovery of his health.

He intends to spend some weeks with your father, as he has an ardent desire to review the scenes of his early childhood, so long forgotten, as well as to see you, my Jane, whom he always mentions with the tenderest affection.

Your father attends him, and desires me to apprize you of it. The Duke with this sends a letter to your mother; prepare, therefore, to receive and admire your royal Cousin; prepare, also, to see again your friend, for my father attends the King, and commands me to accompany him.

Lady Catherine has a favored lover in Lord Herbert, as I imagine you know, and does not yet return.

We both concur in opinion on the character of the Duke of Northumberland; but is not the genius of the times we live in harsh and bloody? Did not even Somerset himself attaint and execute his own brother, Lord Seymour? though I acknowledge not without great provocation; nor was Northumberland's attainder of Somerset unprovoked, who acknowledged that he had employed assassins to murder the Duke.

Let us then, my dear, endeavour to judge impartially; whatever may be the father's character and motives, the son has done nothing to offend; and his love for you is without bounds — he has made me the confident of it, complaining bitterly of your prejudices against his family.

You will be astonished at this, but yet more so, when I tell you that I have seen and conversed with Sir William Morley; that he has revealed to me his passion for your Ladyship, and intreated me to plead with you for him. All this, however strange, is very true; though I am not at liberty to say more at present.

He returns to you in attendance on the King; you will then have this riddle fully unfolded.

Ever your affectionate,
Anne Grey [Lane 53].

Lady Anne hints that she knows more than she may divulge about Sir William Morley, but in the next letter from Lady Jane to her sister Catherine, we read what Anne had been keeping from Lady Jane.

As I find my letters were read to you, my dear sister, I will continue to express my feelings as they arose, and to acquaint you with every thing which has since happened.

It is near a month ago I received that letter from my cousin, which so astonished me; and for nearly a week after, I remained in that state of suspense which her cruelty excited; at the conclusion of which, the arrival of the King put an end to it, in a manner totally unexpected; for after the first transports of our meeting were over, Lady Anne introduced Sir William Morley to me, as Lord Guildford Dudley. Amazement, confusion, joy, a thousand different passions pressed upon my heart at once, and deprived me of speech.

She had contrived that we should be alone at this interview, and Lord Guildford took advantage of my surprise, and the satisfaction which, I suppose, he saw visible in my countenance, to make a declaration of his passion; and, in the most submissive terms, intreated me to forgive the innocent stratagem, which my parents had prevailed on him to join with them in; presuming that he might, by that means, conquer those prejudices which, though unseen, I had conceived against him; and which, they were fearful, would be an everlasting bar to his addresses.

He added, that the king's unexpected visit, and the necessity he was under of going to town, had been rather unfavorable to their design; but that he should be the most miserable of men, if I would not forgive this innocent artifice, and grant him some hopes that I was not totally indifferent to him.

I expressed a little displeasure at being then deceived, but my countenance not being in unison with my tongue, it had but little effect.

Lady Anne, at the same time, introduced to us my parents, who were too much rejoiced in finding their scheme had so well succeeded, to express their feelings. The King was soon informed of this affair, and congratulated us in the most amiable and friendly manner, on the prospect of our future happiness.

I am aware you will say, my Jane, where are your scruples on account of the family of Dudley? Are they all vanished? — I will acknowledge that, with regard to him personally, they are. — His noble mind cannot be guilty of a deliberate crime, of the least injustice. — His virtues compensate fully for his father's faults; and, from the ingenuous sincerity of his temper, and the ardency of his affection to me, I think if happiness is to be found on earth, I may hope for it in a union with him.

I rejoice, my dear sister, that you have an equal prospect of felicity in Lord Herbert: may we endeavor to render ourselves more and more worthy of our happy lot; and to abound in those virtues which may best contribute to the felicity of the Lords to whom we are to be united.

I am, my dear sister,
Yours sincerely,
Jane Grey [Lane 61].

The scheme devised by Guildford's and Jane's parents worked. Jane's strong prejudice against the Dudley family in general would have prevented her from being objective about Guildford had they not deceived her, thus enabling Northumberland's initial plan. The scheme must also have been a topic of conversation between Suffolk and Northumberland, as another letter refers to it.

Lady Jane's next letter to Lady Catherine was likely written in the third week in May, since Jane describes her father's "magnificent preparations" for the dual wedding, hers and Lady Catherine's. Except for Edward's illness, Jane would have been in a wonderful mood.

Our felicity is a good deal interrupted here, my dear sister, by the increasing illness of the royal Edward; but with his complaints, his patience and sweetness also increase; and all his endeavor is to prevent his friends from feeling too sensibly on his account. We have been using every effort to abate the languor that hangs on his sprits, by all the amusements which the place and company could afford: the King has joined in them all, as long as his spirits and strength would permit, and earnestly requests that they may not be shortened when he is obliged to retire from them.

His Majesty is very desirous that our marriage may take place during his presence here, and that yours may also be celebrated at the same time.

My father has ordered magnificent preparations, and intends to go to town, to convey you and Lord Herbert here: everything is to be suitable to my father's rank, and the guest he is honored with. But what have all these things to do with the simple pleasures of the heart? The trappings of grandeur are rather inimical than friendly to real love and friendship, and seem as if furnished by human invention as substitutes to the internal joys of real sentiment and refined sensibility. But though we want not their assistance to complete our felicity, we must acquiesce in them, my Catherine, to oblige our friends.

Adieu, my dear sister, may the hour be propitious that unites us to the men we love, and may the royal Edward soon find returning health, prays

Your

Jane Grey [Lane 67].

As the wedding date of May 21 approached, Edward's physicians announced that he was too weak to attend. Edward's deep affection and high regard for his cousin made his inability to attend difficult for him.

At her wedding, Lady Jane wore a headdress of green velvet, set round with precious stones. She wore a gown of cloth of gold and a mantle of silver tissue. Her hair hung down her back, combed and plaited in a curious fashion then unknown to ladies of quality. This arrangement was said to have been devised by Mrs. Elizabeth Tylney, her friend and attendant, who remained with her to the end. The bride was led to the altar by two handsome pages, with bride lace and rosemary tied to their sleeves. Sixteen virgins, dressed in pure white, preceded the bride to the altar (Lindsay 136-137).

A surviving quotation describes the ceremony as "a gaudy glittering parade conducted, to Ascham's disgust, 'much in the old popish fashion' and he added, which was later to be proved correct, that John Dudley, 'notwithstanding his pretended zeal for the Reformation, was a papist at heart'" (Lindsay 137).

With the magnificent ceremonies over, Lady Jane wrote to Lady Anne about her new life and her grief at the separation from her parents. Lady Jane had always been near her sister, parents, or servants when visiting strange homes, but at the Duke of Northumberland's residence, Durham House, Jane was alone with her new husband for the first time.

> My dear Lady Anne will, I know, rejoice at the increasing felic-ity of her friend. — Lord Guildford is deserving of my highest love and esteem; his character improves on me every day, from the vari-ous opportunities which he has in his own house, and surrounded by his dependents, of displaying the virtues of beneficence and charity, and an earnest desire to promote happiness and comfort every where within his sphere of influence.
>
> The tenderness of his affection for me seems everyday to increase, and the more I discover of his mind and heart, the more earnestly do I seek, by gratitude to God, and every endeavor of improving to my own mind, to consult his happiness, and render myself more deserving of his affection.
>
> The situation of our house is delightful; we have some worthy and agreeable families near us, and every thing around wears a smiling and elegant form; yet hardly can I divest myself of the grief of separation from my beloved parents, from whom I still regret being so far removed, and must flatter myself with the hopes of

seeing them soon; as also Lord Herbert and Lady Catherine. Still, with all this, my happiness will be incomplete, unless the King is better, and I can also enjoy the company of my dear Lady Anne. — Is there not always, my friend, some alloy in human felicity! Can we expect to find it prefect in a state where every thing is mutable?

To you shall I own, that the situation of the King's health, the gloomy prospect of losing him, and Mary's succession, a thousand fears; some of which I cannot account for, will at times, if my Lord is absent from me, intrude into my apprehensive mind: he no sooner re-appears, however, than the cloud vanishes, and hope and joy take possession of my soul.

Take care of your health, my lovely cousin, nor let your extreme sympathy for the excellent Edward wound your heart too deeply.

I wish to hear frequently from you; you know my anxiety to be informed of the state of his Majesty's health as often as is possible.

Adieu,

Jane Grey [Lane 75].

The bliss shared by Lady Jane and Guildford, Lord Herbert and Lady Catherine appears in the next letter, which Lady Anne wrote to a Lady Dudley. She also mentions Edward's illness, and other questions arise from this letter which are not easily answered.

The Lady Dudley to whom Lady Anne Grey addressed the letter was, in all probability, Jane Dudley, the Duchess of Northumberland. Yet it seems odd that Lady Anne would be the first to bear news of the couple's blissful state and that the duchess would be so far removed from her husband's affairs.

Further questions arise from another letter, written on July 7, the day after Edward died, by Lady Dudley to Lady Catherine. In the sixth paragraph, she speaks of "my excellent sister-in-law." The reference is confusing — no known source indicates that John Dudley had a sister, but in fact only two brothers.

Even though Lady Jane was, technically, Jane Dudley, judging by the content it does not make sense that the two letters would have been addressed to her. Research has yielded no other Jane Dudley than the Duchess of Northumberland.

Your friend, Lady Catherine, had commissioned me to inform you, Lady Dudley, that the two amiable pairs are united by the firm bands of mutual love, and the love of their country.

To express the joy of their parents, and the complete delight that appears in themselves, is impossible. So noble and beautiful a pair, as Lord Guildford and Lady Jane, surely never was excelled; and the dignity in every different relation of life, attract to them all hearts, and bind them in the fetters of love and admiration.

Lord Herbert and Lady Catherine are also extremely amiable; the King seemed delighted with their felicity, though his health still declining, will not permit him to share long in mirthful scenes: indeed, I fear he suffers much; and not all the satisfaction I feel at the happiness of my fair cousins, can prevent me from deeply sympathizing in the sufferings of the amiable Edward. He sees my attention to, and solicitude for him, and entreats me to return to town with my father, whither he is soon going, as he tells me my conversation will alleviate his pains, and divert his languor. How happy shall I be may it prove so; with pleasure, therefore, I obey my King, the brother, the friend of my childhood.

He does not propose to travel much farther, as the weather is so warm, and his weakness will not admit of it.

Lord Guildford and Lady Jane, are going to a seat which the Duke has relinquished to them, and Lord Herbert and Lady Catherine remain awhile longer with their parents.

Adieu, my dear Lady Dudley, believe me your's affectionately. Anne Grey [Lane 71].

In early June, Edward's doctors told the Spanish ambassador that the king could not live more than three days; Northumberland's plan depended on the king living longer than that. Though Edward's devise was in rough draft, Northumberland needed to get it completed and passed through Parliament — before Edward died.

Summoned to Greenwich Palace on June 12, the Lord Chief Justice, Sir Edward Montague, the Solicitor-General, and the Attorney General arrived at the bedside of a sickly Edward, still with a persistent cough. Northumberland accompanied the several councilors also present. The judges each knelt at the royal bedside, then waited for the king to speak. In a raspy voice, Edward addressed the judges:

> Our long sickness hath caused us heavily to think of the conditions and prospects of our realm. Should the Lady Mary or the Lady Elizabeth succeed, she might marry a stranger, and the laws and liberties of England be sacrificed, and religion changed. We desire, therefore, that the succession be altered, and we call upon your lordships to receive our command upon the drawing up of this deed by letters patent [Chapman, *The Last Tudor King*, 180]

After the devise was read, the king ordered a deed of settlement drawn upon its articles. Fearfully, the Lord Chief Justice said, "What His Majesty requires is illegal and could not be drawn up under the heading of an act of Parliament" (*op. cit.*, 281).

Coughing and gasping for breath, Edward replied, "I will hear no objections. I command you to draw the letters patent forthwith" (*ibid.*, 281]

The judges realized what their king commanded was illegal; but to refuse to obey him would be treasonous. Therefore, they asked the King for time to review the document. Edward granted their request.

The judges were summoned by the council to Northumberland's palace of Ely Place in Holborn. When Sir Edward Montague asked a member of the council whether he had agreed to sign the devise or not, he responded that he could not do so.

A door flew open, and Northumberland burst in, "trembling for anger; and amongst his ragious talk, called Sir Edward Montague traitor" (Lindsay 141).

The following day, the judges found an angry Edward still confined to his bed but no less in command of the situation. Northumberland was present, and members of the Privy Council surrounded Edwards's bed. Edward asked sharply where his letter patent was and why they had not signed it as he had ordered. He then ordered Sir Edward Montague to "Make quick dispatch," and added that he intended to call a Parliament immediately. Montague, now sobbing, fell to his knees and pleaded with the king: "I have served Your Majesty and Your Majesty's noble father these nineteen years. I am a weak old man without comfort and with nineteen children" (Chapman, *The Last Tudor King*, 282).

Edward, still upset, ignored his pleas and repeated his demand. After much deliberation, they eventually agreed that all who signed the devise would be pardoned; and reluctantly, they signed. By June 21, the judges and the Privy Council had all signed the devise. Some surrendered to Northumberland's intimidation. As a reward to those who gave their support, Northumberland awarded lands and titles (Loach 165).

As the Duke of Northumberland was rejoicing upon completing another step of his plan, perhaps the one he anticipated would be most difficult, Lady Jane wrote a letter to her sister Catherine in the last week of June about the disarray in her own life.

> How much more reason than ever have I to pray for the life of the King! Yet, alas, how little have I to hope it. The ambition of my parents and father-in-law, is about to involve your Jane in a thousand dangers.
>
> The King is worse and worse everyday, and has sent for Lord Guildford and myself to attend him. We immediately quitted our peaceful mansion, where we had formed a thousand plans of future improvement and benevolence, and attended the King. He was rejoiced to see us, and expatiated to me on the attention of Lady Dudley and Lady Anne Grey, and their exertions to assist and amuse him.
>
> He looks exceedingly ill, yet retains the same composed and peaceful frame of mind. But how was I amazed to see my gentle cousin pale, emaciated, evidently suffering by the tenderest sympathy, every pang of her Royal Friend.
>
> I was filled with the deepest regret to see her thus — alas, she knows how deceitful to appearance, and yet how hopeless is Edward's disorder; and, though daily deceived, she is daily flattered by the syren Hope, which her extreme affection for him leads her to form, is spite of her reason.
>
> But I must now proceed to tell you what they have done. They have persuaded the King to set aside his sisters, and declare me his successor to the crown, by the right of my mother, who declines it in my favor.

In vain have I thrown myself at the Royal Edward's feet, incessantly intreating him to drop the design, and destroy the patent; but all my fears, all my endeavors are vain; it is all signed, and was completed before I had the least intimation of it, and they have it in their possession.

My husband joins in the earnest wish of seeing me Queen of England, should we lose the King; and not even a wife, he professes to love so tenderly, can gain the least influence over him on this occasion.

He pleads his father's pleasure — the anxiety that all our families, and, indeed, all the reformed part of the kingdom are in on account of Mary's religion — they use every argument with me, that art or eloquence can invent, to engage my consent to preserve the Protestant cause, and the liberties of the kingdom.

In vain have I urged the injustice of depriving the Princess Elizabeth of her right, an amiable Lady, and a Protestant. They say she was not legitimate, and her father had excluded her for that reason, and that it was Edwards's pleasure to prefer my mother's claim. Why, then, will not my mother herself take on her the weighty burden of the state? Alas, how ill-calculated am I for it! Young, inexperienced in the world, who have been brought up in retirement, and infinitely prefer the joys of a private and domestic life, to all the dangerous and fatiguing glories of greatness.

In vain are all my remonstrance's, all my tears are fruitless, and I have no resource left but to supplicate Heaven to spare Edward's life! and no other employment but to assist, with the rest of the young Nobility around him, by every tender office of friendship, to amuse the wearisome house of sickness and languor.

The King takes short rides every day, and my Guildford and I generally attend him. The conversation, when he can talk, mostly turns on serious subjects; at these seasons, his religion is a steady lamp within him, illuminating the dark shades of declining nature; his sentiments are all noble; his mind submits with a humble acquiescence to the stroke of Heaven; a solicitude for Mary's conversation, and his kingdom's welfare, seem the only things which distress him; though he frequently regrets some instances of persecuting severity, which, during his short and tumultuous reign, he has been almost compelled, by one of the Protectors, to give a reluctant consent to, and which, at the time, cost him many tears. Nor would he ever repeat it, when sole master of his actions, which he then was not, being a minor.

I frequently regretted how much the sprit of persecution has adhered, even to those who have professed the reformed religion, though so contrary to the example of the divine founder of it, for the "wrath of man worketh not the righteousness of God." — Bishop Cranmer, and my uncle Somerset, were not entirely free from it, which I have frequently lamented.

O, my sister, pray for your Jane — pray to Heaven to give her fortitude and strength of mind, to support the various changes of life; and, above all, pray for the King's life; and that some providential event, yet unthought of, may for ever avert from her the snares and perils of royalty, and restore her to the sweet and secure enjoyments of retired and domestic life.

Adieu [Lane 95].

As Edward's illness grew worse with each passing day, the Duke of Northumberland realized he had to keep the king alive long enough to apprehend Princess Mary, who would most certainly assert her claim to the crown. He therefore dismissed the physicians who had tended the king since his birth and replaced them with his own doctor and a woman who claimed she could restore the king's health to "that of normal." Little is known of the woman, though early historians suggest she was a schoolmistress. Disregarding the complaints of Edward's physicians, a woman with no demonstrable professional skill and of unknown reputation gained complete access to the King of England. In days, the remedies she employed began taking a toll on the king. They contained arsenic, in small quantities, which made Edward's hair fall out and darkened his once pale skin. Many questioned the woman's motives and in early July, she was dismissed and never heard from again. Edward's own physicians were then reinstalled. Rumors suggested that the woman was murdered to keep her from disclosing something.

Indeed, rumors abounded, some saying that the Duke of Northumberland and his quack were intentionally poisoning the king. Crowds gathered on July 2 and the following day to see the king, but a gentleman of Edward's bedchamber told them the air was too cold for Edward to visit them.

The rumors of poison and the unorthodox choice of a schoolmistress to treat the king damaged the Duke of Northumberland's reputation tremendously. Whether or not the Duke tried to poison Edward is debatable. A letter written by John Burcher to Henry Bullinger, the protestant leader with whom Jane had corresponded, dated August 16, 1553 and indicating the feelings of many, including "learned men," provides matter for debate.

Greeting. What I wrote in my formal letter, my honored Bullinger, is daily confirmed, and more than confirmed, by the statements of some excellent men. That monster of a man, the Duke of Northumberland, has been committing a horrible and portentous crime. A writer worthy of credit informs me, that our excellent King has been most shamefully taken off by poison. His nails and hair fell off before his death, so that, handsome as he was, he entirely lost all his good looks. The perpetrators of the murder were ashamed of allowing the body of the deceased King to lie in state, and be seen by the public, as is usual: wherefore they buried him privately in a paddock adjoining the palace, and substituted in his place, to be seen by the people, a youth not very unlike him whom they had murdered. One of the sons of the Duke of Northumberland acknowledged this fact. The Duke has been apprehended with his five sons, and nearly twenty persons of rank; among whom is Master Cheke, Doctor Cox, and the Bishop of London, with others unknown to you either by name or reputation. It is thought that these persons gave their consent and sanction, that Jane, the wife of the Duke's son, should be proclaimed Queen: should this prove to be the case, it is all over with them. The King of France has sent word to the city of Calais and to Guisnes, for the citizens to remove, and leave the city and camp at Guisnes at his disposal, for that it was promised him by the English council. The Duke and his fellow prisoners are supposed to have been guilty of this shameful deed. Forces are collecting in England to defend the city and territory. I am afraid lest your Swiss should be sent against us. You see, my dear friend, how you are deprived of all your expectation respecting our England: you must consider therefore what you should determine upon respecting your son. My house is open to him, and my services shall not be wanting. Farewell, and diligently, I pray you, salute all your learned men. I am exceedingly obliged to you all for the kindness you have shewn me.

Yours, BURCHER. [Robinson 104].

Between eight and nine o'clock on the evening of July 6, Edward died, in the presence of his doctors. The King is said to have died in Sidney's arms, uttering these last words: "I am faint: Lord have mercy upon me, and take my spirit." And so, as Chapman observes, England lost the last Tudor king (285).

Edward's death was kept a secret, just as his father's had been. Preparations had to be made for implementing the change in succession and for Jane to take her place on the throne.

The Duke of Northumberland faced yet another problem: what to do with Edward's body. An autopsy preceding the embalming might reveal symptoms confirming the use of poison. Early historians have suggested that the bones now lying beneath the altar of the Chapel of Henry VIII in Westminster Abbey are not Edward's but in fact those of a young boy who looked like him. No evidence remains to substantiate this claim, and without a statement by someone who was close to the events surrounding Edward's death, the fate of his body remains a mystery.

A second letter from Lady Dudley to Jane's sister Lady Catherine raises several questions, as well. The letter is in two parts; the first is easily dated to July 7, the day after Edward died, and the second is perhaps from July 9.

> How shall I unfold, to my dear Lady Catherine, the melancholy news of the King's death! — He expired yesterday, to the extreme affliction of all his friends.
>
> Your sister, and Lady Anne, are utterly incapable of writing, which have requested me to do, being more composed: my pen is unable to paint the affecting interviews between them.
>
> Lord Guildford was beloved by his King with the sincerest friendship, and moans his loss with unaffected sorrow: they have all paid him the strictest attention, and watched over him like a mother over a dying child.

The patience, the gratitude, the piety which the King displayed throughout his last trying scene, has completed the beauty of his character, and will leave an endless regret for his early fate, in the hearts of all his friends and faithful subjects.

Lady Jane is appointed his successor to the throne. — Alas! amiable Lady Jane — I fear greatly for her, from the princess Mary's adherents. — The King's death is not yet made public — the Duke of Northumberland, and the Council, have sent for the Princesses to see their brother, with the design of getting them into their power. — How much artifice, how much injustice does ambition occasion!

My excellent sister-in-law still incessantly prays her parents to retire to France, and leave the crown to the rightful successor; but their ambition renders them immovable. — Lord Guildford also, amiable as he is in every other respect, refuses her earnest request to quit them all, and fly with her.

As soon as the Princesses are secured, Lady Jane is to be proclaimed Queen of England. — Ah! my dear Lady, how many thorns will be concealed among the jewels of thy crown! — I tremble for thee, good and noble, and worthy as thou art to wear and adorn it.

My mind, too much warped, perhaps, to melancholy, from the bloody events of my family, which are within my remembrance, feels a portending gloom.

All nature seems enwrapt in a still, sable cloud of suspensive horror, as if big with some great event. — The silence diffused through the palace; Lady Jane's deep affliction; the solicitous, and important looks of the Protector and Council, for their success with the people, by whom you know the Dudley's are but little beloved; their fears of the Princesses party; altogether, render this a most solemn moment.

For my part, I know not what to pray for; either their success or disappointment: their success, in my opinion, would be founded in injustice; and yet, their failure, and the Princess Mary's succession to the crown would, without doubt, involve the nation in a thousand miseries, and be the ruin of our family and party. — The overthrow of the Reformation would be inevitable, bigoted as that Princess is to the Popish religion; and I tremble lest the innocent Jane should be the victim of her fury.

We are to quit the palace, as soon as the messenger returns from the Princesses. — I will not close my letter till then, as I have a save conveyance for it to you, which I may not again meet with — till then, adieu.

O, my dear Lady Catherine, too true, indeed, were my portents. — Mary had, by some means, been informed of her brother's decease; she privately left her abode, and has fled to the county of Suffolk, from whence, in all probability, she will return with an army, as the people seem more attached to her than it was imagined they would.

No sooner did the Duke receive the news, than he immediately got Lady Jane proclaimed, and conveyed to the Tower for safety, as is usual on these occasions; thither we all attended her: but I cannot express the reluctance with which she accepted of the crown; and nothing at last could prevail on her to consent, but the pressing entreaties of her parents and husband; who threw themselves on their knees before her, and made the most affecting remonstrance's in their power to her, in behalf of the Protestant cause, and the happiness of the people.

To these considerations, and her duty to her parents, she has yielded up her own peace and happiness, and all that sincere and heartfelt delight, which she experienced from the innocence and usefulness of her private and domestic life, which rendered her an ornament to society, and the idol of her friends and relations.

Lady Anne and myself accompany her, and will transmit to you an account of every event of importance that occur to us.

My dear Lady Catherine, shall we not soon see you in town? you have now, you know, a new duty to pay, since your sister is a queen. — Alas, how little is her title to be envied!

I am ever your sincere friend,

Jane Dudley [Lane 104].

Lady Dudley's surprise at Jane's appointment and her concern for Jane's fate seem to go against all one would assume about the Duchess' knowledge of, if not involvement in, her husband's affairs. Perhaps further information will be discovered to help elucidate the matter.

CHAPTER 2. REIGNING PERIOD

On July 8, 1553, the Lord Mayor, with six aldermen, six "merchants of the staple, and as many merchant adventurers," were summoned to Greenwich and there were secretly informed of the king's death and of his will by letters patent, "to which they were sworn and charged to keep it secret" (Taylor 217).

On the same day, the council sent a letter to Sir Philip Hoby, Ambassador to the Holy Roman Empire and to Flanders, announcing King Edward's death.

> After our hearty Commendations. We must needs be sorry at that which cometh both from us, and goeth to you, with such extreme Sorrow, as the like never passed under these our Hands. But such is the Almighty Will of God in all his Creatures, that his Order in Time may not be by us resisted. In one word, we must tell you a great heap of Infelicity: God hath called out of this World our Sovereign Lord, the sixth of this Month, towards Night. Whose manner of Death was such, toward God, as assureth us, that his Soul is in Place of eternal Rest. His Disease whereof he died, was of the Putrefaction of the Lungs, being utterly uncure-able of this Evil. For the Importance we advertise you, knowing it to have [been]most Comfort to have been thereof ignorant. And the same ye may take Time to defer to the Emperor, as from us,

who know assuredly, that his Majesty will sorrow and condole with us, for the Departure and Loss of a Prince of that Excellency, and so dear a Brother and Friend: Not doubting but that his Majesty will have in Remembrance the ancient Amity that hath been always betwixt their Ancestors. For consideration whereof, ye shall assure him, that there shall not be any thing lacking on our Parts, but all readiness to observe and maintain the same. And so we wish to us all the Comfort of God's Spirit in all Adversities.

July 8, 1553 [Strype 430].

Another letter written the same day was addressed to the French king. Mr. Lodge dates the letter July 8, 1553, in his *Illustrations of British History, Biography, and Manners, in the Reigns of Henry VIII, Edward VI, Mary, Elizabeth, and James I*, though there is no date on the document itself. A note preceding this letter in Mr. Lodge's book suggests that the documents are rough drafts of letters from the Privy Council to the English ambassadors at the French and imperial courts.

LORDS *of the* COUNCIL *to*

After our hearty commendations. We must need be sorry now to write that which come both sorrowfully from us, and shall, we well know, with the like sorrow be taken of you; but such is the almighty will of God in all his creations, that his order in them may not be by us resisted: In one word we must tell you a great heap of infelicity: God hath called out of this world our Sovereign Lord the sixth of this month; whose manner of death was such toward God as assure us his soul is in the place of eternal joy, as for your own satisfaction party you may perceive by the copy of the words which he spoke secretly to himself at the moment of his death. The disease where of his Majesty died was the disease of the lungs, which had in them two great ulcers, and were putrefied, by means where of he fell into a consumption, and so hath he wasted, being utterly incurable. Of this evil, for the importance, we advise you, knowing it most comfortable to have been ignorant of it; and the same you may take time to declare unto the Emperor, as from us, which know assuredly that as his Majesty will sorrow with us and this realm the departure and loss of a Prince of such excellence, and so dear a brother and friend to him and countries; not doubting but his majesty will have in remembrance the ancient amities that hath been always between this realm of England and the house of Burgundy, and other his majesties dominions; for conservation where of you shall assure his that there shall not be any lack found of our part, but always a readiness to observe and maintain the same, for the weal of both the nations.

TO Ye FRENCH

And in the end ye shall declare that his Majesties Ambassadors have here showed unto us that which he had in charge from his M^r, by his l^{res}, touching the detection of certain practices of the Emperor intended with the Lady Mary, to the daughter of this realm, for the avoiding where of his Majesty, like a place of great honor, offerth such help as he may conveniently; where surely his majesty show himself so worldly of praise and thanks, of us and all this realm, as we shall never forget this his great friendship in so difficult times, although we doubt not but that the estate and power of this realm shall, by God's goodness, prevail against all manner of practices or attempts, either by the Emperor or any other, either foreign or outward enemies, whatsoever the same be [Lodge 182-183].

The following day, Sir John Gates summoned the palace guard, informed them of the king's death and of his will, and desired them to swear their allegiance to Queen Jane and to the crown of England. He further explained that the Lady Mary was not fit to succeed for three reasons: her mother's divorce from Henry VIII, her Catholicism, and her sex.

Mary, now at Kenninghall, received the grave news of her brothers' death, presumably from an informant loyal to her, though great care had been taken to restrict the news to those directly involved. Assuming that she was to accept that which her father had indicated in his will, she wrote a letter to the lords of the Council on July 9, asserting her claim to the crown and noting how "strange" it was for them not to have notified her of the tragic news immediately. The princess was clearly ready to claim the crown and signified that to the lords.

My Lords, We Greet You well; and have received sure Advertisement, that Our Dearest Brother, the King, Our late Sovereign
Lord, is departed to God's Mercy. Which News how woeful they
be unto Our Heart, He only knoweth, to whose Will, and Pleasure, We must, and do humbly submit Us, and Our Wills. But, in
this so lamentable a Case, that is, to wit, after His Majesties
Departure, and Death, concerning the Crown, and Governance of
this Realm of England, with the Title of France, and all things
thereto belonging; what hath been provided by Act of Parliament,
and the Testament, and Last Will of Our Dearest Father, besides
other Circumstances Advancing Our Right; You know, the Realm,
and the whole World knoweth: the Rolls, and Records appear, by
the Authority of the King, Our said Father, and the King, Our said
Brother, and the Subjects of this realm. So that We verily trust,
that there is no good true Subject, that is, can, or would pretend to
be ignorant thereof: And of Our part, We have of Our Selves
caused, and as God shall aid, and strengthen Us, shall cause, Our
Right, and Title in this behalf, to be Published, and Proclaimed
accordingly. And albeit this so Weighty a Matter seemeth strange,
that the Dying of our said Brother, upon Thursday at night, last
past, We hitherto had no knowledge from You thereof; yet we
consider your Wisdom, and Prudence to be such, that having
often amongst You Debated, Pondered, and well Weighted this
present Case, with Our Estate, Your Own Estate, the Common
Wealth, and all Our Honors; We shall and may conceive Great
Hope, and Trust, with much assurance in Your Loyalty, and Service; and therefore for the time interpret, and take things, not to
the worst, that Ye yet will, like Noble Men, Work the best. Nevertheless We are not ignorant of Your Consultations; to Undo the
Provisions made for Our Preferment; nor of the Great Hands, and
Provisions forcible, wherewith You be Assembled, and Prepared:
by whom, and to what end, God, and You know; and Nature cannot, but fear some Evil. But be it, that some Consideration Politic,
or whatsoever thing else, hath moved You thereto; yet doubt ye
not, My Lords, but We can take all these Your doings, in Gracious
Parts; being also Right-Ready to remit, and fully Pardon the same;
and that to Eschew Bloodshed, and Vengeance, against all those,
that can, or will intend the same; trusting also assuredly, that Ye
will take, and accept this Grace, and Venture in Good Part as
appertaineth; and that We shall not be Enforced to use the Service
of other Our True Subjects, and Friends: which in this Our Just,

and Right Cause, God in whom all Our affiance is shall send Us Wherefore, My Lords, We require You, and charge you, and every of You, of Your allegiance, which You owe to God, and Us, and to none other: for of Our Honor, and the Surety of Our Person, only employ Your Selves; and forthwith, upon receipt hereof, cause Our Right, and Title to the Crown, and Governance of this Realm, to be Proclaimed in Our City of London, and other places, as to your Wisdoms shall seem Good, and as to this Case appertaineth; not failing hereof, as Our very Trust is in You. And this Our Letter, Signed with Our Hand, shall be your sufficient Warrant in that behalf.

Given under Our Signet, at Our Manor of Kenning-Hall, the ninth of July, 1553 [Heylyn 157].

Upon receipt of Mary's letter, the lords responded in a letter dated July 9, rejecting her claim to the crown and asserting the actual investure of "Our Sovereign Lady Queen Jane" and further indicating that Mary should remain "quiet and obedient." The letter was signed by twenty-one councilors and clearly indicated their allegiance to Queen Jane.

Madam,

We have received your letters, the ix of this instant, declaring your supposed title, which you judge yourself to have to the Imperial Crown of this realm, and all the dominions thereunto belonging. For answer whereof, this is to advertise you, that for as much as our Sovereign Lady Queen Jane, is, after the death of our Sovereign Lord Edward VI., a prince of most noble memory; invested and possessed with the just and right title in the Imperial Crown of this realm, not only by good order of old ancient laws of this realm, but also by our late Sovereign Lord's Letters Patent, signed with his own hand, and sealed with the great seal of England, in presence of the most part of the nobles, counselors, judges, with divers other grave and sage personages assenting and subscribing to the same. We must therefore, as of most bound duty and allegiance, assent unto her said Grace, and to none other; except we should, which faithful subjects cannot, fall into grievous and unspeakable enormity, wherefore we can no less do, but for the quiet both of the realm and you, also to advertise you, that forasmuch as the divorce made between the King of famous memory, K.

Henry VIII., and the Lady Katherine your mother, was necessary to be had both by the everlasting laws of God, and also by ecclesiastical laws, and also by the most part of the noble and learned universities of Christendom, and confirmed also by the sundry acts of Parliament remaining yet in their force, and thereby you justly made illegitimate and uninheritable to the Crown Imperial of this realm, and the rules, dominions, and possessions of the same, you will upon just consideration hereof, and of divers other causes, lawful to be alleged for the same, and for the just inheritance of the right line and godly orders, taken by the late King, our Sovereign Lord King Edward VI., and agreed upon by the nobles and greatest personages aforesaid, surcease by any pretence to vex and molest any of our Sovereign Lady Queen Jane, her subjects, from their true faith and allegiance due unto her Grace: assuring you, that if you will for respect show yourself quiet and obedient, as you ought, you shall find us all several ready to do you any service that we with duty may, and be glad with your quietness to preserve the common state of this realm, wherein you may be otherwise grievous unto us, to yourself, and to them. And thus we bid you most heartily well to fare. From the Tower of London, this ix of July, 1553.

Your Ladyship's friends, shewing yourself an obedient subject.

Thomas Canterbury,	Huntington,
The Marques of Winchester,	Darcy,
John Bedford,	Cheyny,
W. Northampton,	R. Cotton,
Thomas Ely, Chancellor,	John Gates,
Northumberland,	W. Peter,
Henry Suffolk,	W. Cicelle,
Henry Arundel,	John Cheke,
Shrewsbury,	John Mason,
Pembroke,	Edw. North,
Cobham,	E. Bows,
R. Ritch [Nicolas 68].	

That same day the council, completely subjugated and terrorized by Northumberland, decided to proclaim Lady Jane queen. Mary Sidney was chosen and sent to Jane while she was at

Chelsea. The two girls were to take a water barge to Syon House and wait there.

Northumberland preceded the councilors into the room where Mary Sidney and Lady Jane waited. Two lords engaged Jane in conversation, perhaps to prepare her for the official announcement. "With unwonted caresses," she says, "they did me such reverence as was not at all suitable to my state" [Chapman, Lady Jane Grey, 103].

Doubtless, she was bewildered by the attention paid her, since she was unaware that Edward had already died.

The Duke of Northumberland then requested that Jane and Mary Sidney proceed with him and the lords to the Chamber of State, where she found her parents, husband, mother-in-law, and Lady Northampton, who all did her reverence. The duke led the confused and possibly frightened Jane to a dais under the canopy reserved for royal personages.

Numerous accounts of the following events exist. Peter Heylyn's 1661 *History of the Reformation of the Church of England* used sources just over a hundred years old and is likely more accurate than many, if not most.

> The Duke of Northumberland informed her that; That the King was dead, and that he had declared her for his next successor in the crown imperial; that this declaration was approved by all the lords of the council, most of the peers, and all the judges of the land, which they had testified by the subscription of their names, and all this ratified and confirmed by letters patents, under the great seal of England; that the lord mayor, the alderman, and some of the principle citizens had been spoke withal, by whom they were assured of the fidelity of the rest of the city; that there was nothing wanting but her grateful acceptance of the high estate, which God almighty, the sovereign disposer of all crowns, and scepters, (never sufficiently to be thanked by her, for so great a mercy) had advanced her to that therefore she should cheerfully take upon her, the name, title, and estate of Queen of England, France and Ireland, with all the royalties, and preeminence's to the same belonging; receiving at their hands the first fruits of the humble duty (now tendered by them on their knees) which

shortly was to be played to her, by the rest of the kingdom [Hey-lyn 159].

Sir Peter reports that after Northumberland's speech Lady Jane found herself in a great perplexity, not knowing whether to lament the death of the king or to rejoice at her adoption of the kingdom. Heylyn says Jane viewed the crown as a great temptation and took some time, therefore, in deliberation. After considering matters, she tearfully answered:

> That the laws of the Kingdom, and natural right, standing for the King's sister[s], she would beware of burthening her weak conscience with a yoke, which did belong to them; that she under-stood the infamy of those, who had permitted the violation of right to gain a scepter; that it were to mock God, and deride jus-tice, to scruple at the stealing of a shilling, and not at the usurpa-tion of a crown. Besides I am not so young, nor so little read in the guiles of fortune, to suffer my self to be taken by them. If she enrich any, it is but to make them the subject of her spoil, if she raise others, it is but to pleasure herself with their ruins. What she adored yesterday, is today her pastime. And, if I now permit her to adorn, and crown me, I must tomorrow suffer her to crush, and tear me in pieces. Nay with what crown doth she present me. A crown, which hath been violently and shamefully wrestled from Katherine of Aragon; made more unfortunate by the punishment of Ann Boleyn, and others, that wore it after her. And why then would you have me add my blood to theirs, and to be the third vic-tim, from whom this fatal crown may be ravished with the head that wears it? But in case it should not prove fatal unto me, and that all its venom were consumed; if fortune should give me war-ranties of her constancy: should I be well advised to take upon me these thorns, which would dilacerate, though not kill me outright; to burthen my self with a yoke, which would not fail to torment me, though I were assured not to be strangled with it? My liberty is better, then the chain you proffer me, with what precious stones soever it be adorned, or of what gold soever framed. I will not exchange my peace for honorable and precious jealousies, for mag-nificent and glorious letters. And, if you love me sincerely, and in good earnest, you will rather wish me a secure, and quiet fortune, though mean, then an exalted conditions exposed to the wind, and followed by some dismal fall" [Heylyn 159-160].

Jane did not yield to Northumberland's intimidating tactics easily, and only after a long delay did she finally concede. "If what hath been given to me is lawfully mine, may thy Divine Majesty grant me such spirit and grace that I may govern to Thy glory and service, to the advantage of this realm" (Taylor 106).

Soon afterwards, she was proclaimed Queen of England, with the usual formalities. England had a new Queen, and a letter was issued the same day, July 10, indicating Lady Jane's accession to the throne.

Jane by the Grace of God, Queen of *England, France, and Ireland,* Defender of the Faith, and of the Church of *England,* and also of *Ireland,* under Christ in Earth the supreme Head. To all our most Loving, Faithful, and Obedient Subjects, and to every of them, Greeting. Whereas our most dear Cousin *Edward* the 6th, late King of *England, France,* and *Ireland,* Defender of the Faith; and in Earth, Supreme Head, under Christ, of the Church of *England,* and *Ireland;* by his Letters Patents, signed with his own Hand, and sealed with his Great Seal of *England,* bearing date the 21st day of June, in the seventh Year of his Reign; in the presence of the most part of his Nobles, his Councellors, Judges, and divers other grave and sage Personages, for the profit and surety of the whole Realm, thereto assenting and subscribing their Names to the same, hath, by the same his Letters Patents; recited, That forasmuch as the Imperial Crown of this Realm, by an Act made in the 35th Year of the Reign of the late King, of worthy memory, King *Henry* the 8th, our Progenitor, and great Uncle, was, for lack of issue of his Body lawfully begotten; and for lack of Issue of the Body of our said late Cousin King *Edward* the 6th, by the same Act, limited and appointed to remain to the Lady *Mary* his eldest Daughter, and to the Heirs of her Body lawfully begotten: and for default of such Issue, the Remainder thereof to the Lady *Elizabeth,* by the Name of the Lady *Elizabeth* his second Daughter, and to the Heirs of her Body lawfully begotten; with such Conditions as should be limited and appointed by the said late King of worthy memory, King *Henry* the 8th, our Progenitor, our Great Uncle, by his Letters Patent under his Great Seal, or by his last Will in writing, signed with his Hand. And forasmuch as the said Limitation of the Imperial Crown of this Realm being limited, as is afore-said, to the said Lady Mary and Lady Elizabeth, being illegitimate, and not lawfully begotten, for that the Marriage had, between the said late King, King Henry the 8th, our Progenitor, and Great Uncle, and the Lady *Katherine*, Mother to the said Lady *Mary*; and also the marriage had between the said late King, King *Henry* the 8th, our Progenitor, and Great Uncle, and the Lady *Ann*, Mother to the said Lady *Elizabeth*, were clearly and lawfully undone, by Sentences of Divorce, according to the Word of God, and the Ecclesiastical Laws; and which said several Divorcements, have been severely [sic]ratified and confirmed by Authority of Parliament, and especially in the 28th Year of the reign of the King *Henry* the 8th, our said Progenitor, and Great Uncle, remaining in force, strength, and effect, whereby, as well the said Lady *Mary*, as also the said Lady *Elizabeth*, to all Intents and Purposes, are, and [have] been clearly disabled, to ask, claim, or challenge the said Imperial Crown, or any other of the Honors, Castles, Manors, Lordships, Lands, Tenements, or other Hereditaments, as Heir or Heirs to our said late Cousin King Edward the 6th, or as Heir or heirs to any other Person or Persons whatsoever, as well for the Cause before rehearsed, as also for that the said Lady *Mary*, and Lady *Elizabeth*, were unto our said late Cousin but of the half Blood, and therefore by the Ancient Laws, Statutes, and Customs of this Realm, be not inheritable unto our said late Cousin, although they had been born in lawful Matrimony; as indeed they were not, as by the said Sentences of Divorce, and the said Statute of the 28th Year of the reign of King *Henry* the 8th, our said Progenitor, and Great Uncle, plainly appeareth. And forasmuch also, as it is to be thought, or at the least much to be doubted, that if the said Lady *Mary*, of Lady *Elizabeth*, should hereafter have, or enjoy the said Imperial Crown of this Realm, and should then happen to marry with any Stranger born out of this Realm, that then the said Stranger, having the Government and Imperial Crown in his Hands, would adhere and practice, not only to bring this Noble, Free Realm into the Tyranny and Servitude of the Bishops of *Rome*, but also to have the Laws and Customs of his or their own Native Country or Countries, to be practiced and put in ure within this Realm, rather than the Laws, Statues, and Customs here of long time used; whereupon the Title of Inheritance, of all and singular the Subjects of this Realm do depend, to the peril of Conscience, and the utter subversion of the Common-Weal of this Realm: Whereupon our said late Dear Cousin, weighing and considering within himself, which ways and means were most convenient to be had for the stay of the said Succession, in the said

Imperial Crown, if it should please God to call our said late Cousin out of this transitory Life, having no Issue of his Body. And calling to his remembrance, that We, and the Lady *Katherine*, and the Lady *Mary*, our Sisters, (being the Daughters of the Lady *Frances*, our natural Mother, and then, and yet, Wife to our natural and most loving Father, *Henry* Duke of *Suffolk*; and the Lady *Margaret*, Daughter of the Lady *Eleanor*, then deceased, Sister to the said Lady *Frances*, and the late Wife of our Cousin *Henry* Earl of *Cumberland*) were very nigh of his Grace's Blood, of the part of his Father's side, our said Progenitor, and Great Uncle; and being naturally born here, within the Realm. And for the very good Opinion our said late Cousin had of our said Sisters and Cousin *Margaret's* good Education, did therefore, upon good deliberation and advice herein had, and taken, by his said Letters Patents, declare, order, assign, limit, and appoint, that if it should fortune himself, our said late Cousin King *Edward* the Sixth, to decease, having no Issue of his Body lawfully begotten, that then the said Imperial Crown of *England* and *Ireland* and the Confines of the same, and his Title to the Crown of the Realm of *France*; and all and singular Honors, Castles, Prerogatives, Privileges, Preheminencies, and Authorities, Jurisdictions, Dominions, Possessions, and Hereditaments, to our said late Cousin K. *Edward* the Sixth, or to the said Imperial Crown belonging, or in any wise appertaining, should, for lack of such Issue of his Body, remain, come, and be to the eldest Son of the Body of the said Lady *Frances*, lawfully begotten, being born into the World in his Lifetime, and to the Heirs Males of the Body of such eldest Son lawfully begotten; and so from Son to Son, as he should be of vicinity of Birth of the Body of the said Lady *Frances*, lawfully begotten, being born into the World in our said late Cousin's Life-time, and to the Heir Males of the Body of every such Son lawfully begotten. And for default of such Son born into the World in his life-time, of the Body of the said Lady *Frances*, lawfully begotten; that then the said Imperial Crown, and all and singular other the Premises, should remain, come, and be to us, by the Name of the Lady *Jane*, eldest Daughter of the said Lady Frances and to the Heirs Males of our Body lawfully begotten, and for lack of such Issue, then to the Lady *Katherine* aforesaid, our said second Sister, and the Heirs Male of her Body lawfully begotten, with divers other Remainders, as by the same Letters Patents more plainly and at large it may and doth appear. Sithence the making of our Letters Patents, that is to say, on *Thursday*, which was the 6th day of this instant Month of *July*, it hath pleased God to call unto his infinite Mercy, our said most dear and entirely beloved Cousin, *Edward* the Sixth, whose Soul God pardon; and forasmuch as he is now deceased, having no Heirs of his Body begotten; and that also there remaineth at this present time no Heirs lawfully begotten, of the Body of our said Progenitor, and great Uncle, King *Henry* the Eighth; And forasmuch also as the said Lady *Frances*, our said Mother, had no Issue Male begotten of her Body, and born into the World, in the life-time of our said Cousin King *Edward* the Sixth, so as the said Imperial Crown, and other the Premises to the same belonging, or in any wise appertaining, now be, and remain to us, in our Actual and Royal Possession, by Authority of the said Letters Patents: We do therefore by these Presents signify, unto all our most loving, faithful, and obedient Subjects, That like as we for our part shall, by God's Grace, shew our Self a most gracious and benign Sovereign Queen and Lady to all our good Subjects, in all their just and lawful Suits and Causes; and to the uttermost of our Power, shall preserve and maintain God's most Holy Word, Christian Policy, and the good Laws, Customs, and Liberties of these our Realms and Dominions: so we mistrust not, but they, and every of them, will again, for their parts, at all Times, and in all Cases, shew themselves unto Us, their natural Liege Queen and Lady, most faithful, loving, and obedient Subjects, according to their bounden Duties and Allegiance, whereby they shall please God, and do the things that shall tend to their own preservation and sureties; willing and commanding all Men, of all Estates, Degrees, and Conditions, to see our Peace and accord kept, and to be obedient to our Laws, as they tender our Favor, and will answer for the contrary at their extreme Perils. In witness whereof, we have caused these our Letters to be made Patents. Witness our Self, at our *Tower* of *London*, the tenth day of *July*, in the first Year of our Reign.

God save the Queen [Nicolas 60].

With the official ceremonies past, the reality of her situation at hand and her duties as queen settled upon Jane, and life in the Tower began to follow a routine that rulers before her had followed for several centuries. One matter Jane addressed as soon as time permitted was a review of the prisoners then in the Tower. She reviewed each individual case and in some instances granted liberty.

There were two individuals in particular whom Lady Jane regarded highly.

In a letter from Lady Anne to Lady Catherine, Anne mentioned a Courtney, son of the Marquis of Exeter. He was Edward Courtenay, son of Henry Courtenay and a great-grandson of Edward IV. Henry served with the Duke of Suffolk during the Pilgrimage of Grace uprisings, which broke out over much of northern England in October 1536. Henry was executed in 1538 for his part in a conspiracy to raise men in Devon and Cornwall. Later the Earl of Devon, Courtney remained a prisoner in the Tower for about half his adult life. Mary granted him liberty as soon as she took the throne. Courtenay's name is linked to Mary as a proper suitor for marriage. History has recorded much about the man, who was about twenty-seven years old at Lady Jane's accession. Many accounts describe him as a bumbling buffoon, though he came from a dignified bloodline.

Lady Anne also mentioned a Lady Laurana de M-, the second of two prisoners Jane reviewed. Though there are clues to her identity, she is obscure. She was possibly from the Medici family.

Lady Anne's letter and others hint at a liaison between Courtenay and Laurana, though nothing appears in the many accounts of his life to corroborate the suggestion. Several unnamed women figure in those accounts, especially after Mary's accession and marriage to Philip. Since Courtenay for a while was a potential suitor to Mary, he would have wanted to keep quiet any liaison with Laurana during their imprisonment.

> Your sister, my Catherine, acquits herself, in her exalted situation, with the same humility and affability as in private life. There is in her noble air, a seriousness which seems to arise from the apprehension of insecurity in her new dignity, and a painful idea of not holding it by a lawful claim. This indeed, she has frequently expressed, but her father and friends endeavor to reassure her.
>
> As soon as she was at liberty from the multitude of cares and business, which she was at once involved in, she enquired what prisoners were in the Tower, and ordered them to be brought to

her in turn, that she might attend to their claims. Many amongst them she heard, and set at liberty.

The Duke of Norfolk, and Courtney, son of the Marquis of Exeter, were at last introduced to her. Her tender and compassionate heart was melted at the sight of the venerable Norfolk, attained, as he had been, by Harry the VIIIth on no crime, but his superior family honors and greatness, and being one of the first Noblemen in the kingdom.

How many years had he been immured here, lost to the world and his country; as had also the young and amiable Courtney, who possess a most elegant person and gentle manners, but, being confined so young, appeared ignorant of many accomplishments necessary to a young nobleman; an air of dejection, mixed with resignation, sat on his pale countenance, the sensibility and dignity of which prepossessed all hearts in his favor. He was, also, committed without any crime of his own, when his father was attained.

An amiable and pleasing Lady was next presented, by the desire of Courtenay, who professed himself deeply interested in her welfare. When she was introduced to the Queen, and, after her first address to her, on looking round the room, she suddenly became faint, and was falling down, when I perceived her emotion, which, I thought, proceeded from her discovering Courtney among the company; but every one else, I believe, imputed it to the effects of sickness, which her countenance evidently wore the traces of.

She soon, however, recovered her spirits, and said, she was imprisoned by Bishop Cranmer's Councils to the Protector, in the beginning of Edward's reign, and also a mother, who was since dead; that her crime was an adherence to her religion, which was the Catholic.

The noble freedom with which she acknowledged this, pleased Lady Jane, as it did me, and we entreated the Duke of Suffolk to permit her to remain with us, which he willingly consented to; at the same time saying, that the Lady was at liberty, whenever she chose, to quit the Tower. But the Duke of Norfolk and Courtney were not permitted to enjoy that liberty, till the new Queen was a little more established, though they had leave to walk where they pleased within the Tower walls.

As soon as we were alone with the lovely Lady Laurana de M-, I entreated her to inform us of the principle incidents of her life, if it was not disagreeable to her; that the young nobleman, who had last been examined, professed himself interested warmly in her happiness, and that I had observed they both seemed much affected at their meeting in the Queen's presence, though respect for her had kept them silent, or some other motive to me unknown.

Tears of sensibility filled her eyes at my request, and flowed down her pale cheek, on which dejection had deeply preyed.

After a little pause, she said, she was much obliged to me for the concern I took in her affairs, and would most willingly comply with my request, which she immediately did.

Lady Laurana's story

My family is Italian, and noble, of the house of M-. My parents had some years been settled in England, having quitted their own city, Florence, on account of a tragical family event, which had given them a disgust to it, and wounded their hearts too deeply to permit them again to reside in it.

I was their only child, and brought up in their faith. At length my father died, and my mother still continued here, living as the gentry of this kingdom, but not in a splendid or conspicuous manner, for the greatly preferred retirement.

In the beginning of Edward's reign, the kingdom was divided with religious disputes, which were carried on with such violence and inveteracy, that the spirit of persecution was very prevalent even among Protestants, though they greatly condemned the Catholics for it; and the Protector was too much guided by Bishop Cranmer, in imprisoning, and frequently punishing with torture, those who differed from them, in matters which were deemed by each party essential; so that even women did not escape their tyranny. Amongst the rest my mother and myself, young as I then was, not more than twelve years old, were imprisoned for our obstinacy in our principles.

Thus you see, Madam, that my heart has early learnt to suffer. While my mother lived, however, it was tolerable to me; her conversation and instructions, in every part of education, which she was completely accomplished in, filled up [a] great part of our time. We had a guitar, with some music and other books, which we studied till we had them by heart; and being permitted sometimes to take a little air, the confinement seemed to me so much like that of a nunnery, that it did not cost me my cheerfulness; and my mother endeavoured to maintain her's, that she might render my lot more tolerable. — But, alas! at the end of four years, my dear mother died, after a lingering illness, occasioned, doubtless, by her misfortunes, and the regrets she felt on my account, which, as she carefully kept them from [me], injured her health still more effectually.

I had watched over her with unremitting attention, during her tedious decay; but, when I found she was gone for ever, my grief was so violent and excessive, that they could scarcely tear me away from the insensible body, which I fondly hung over, and suffered more than it is in the power of language to describe in the contemplation of. They conveyed me into another apartment, in a very different part of the Tower.

For a while I gave myself up to sorrow, nor could any thing divert my attention from it; but I sat stupid and unemployed by any of my former avocations. For some months I continued in this way; looking out at my little grated window was the only amusement I took.

The anxieties of my mind were, at length, by slow degrees, relieved, by the voice of a young man confined in the next apartment to mine. At first I paid little attention to him; and if I did, it was with a disgust, as music but ill-accorded with my grief. But, by degrees, as it abated, I began to listen to him, by way of amusement.

It was a long time before I had the pleasure of seeing him; but the sound of his voice was familiar to me, both in singing and reading, which he always did aloud, frequently poetry, which he recited with a great deal of taste and judgment.

I had formed a pleasing idea of him, from the knowledge I had of his sentiments: he would frequently, in his poetry, lament, in the most pathetic manner, the loss of liberty; being shut up from the charms of society, the difficulty which he had to obtain knowledge and improvement of mind, and the desire of those endearing family connections which blest his childhood; then would he solace his mind with the reflection, that the tyranny of others, and not his own guilt, had occasioned this long confinement, which gave him still a hope that Providence would, some way or other, procure the means of his deliverance.

He too well painted his own lot, not to penetrate my heart with a lively sense of his grief, as well as his merit; and, indeed, these amusements were the only ones which I enjoyed.

I received great improvement from the books he read, which were frequently on learned and studious subjects; sometimes religious; from these last, I found he was of the Romish church.

It was near three months, that this invisible youth entertained me daily, unconscious of the pleasure he gave. One day, looking out at my window, I saw a young man walking in a little garden, into which it looked; the dignity of his air, and the elegance of his person, though in disabille, excited my attention. I had frequently seen people walking there, but none had ever gained from me a moment's notice. I secretly wished this might be the unknown person, who had so greatly gained upon my esteem and sympathy.

As he walked, he cast his eyes up at the windows, and at last fixed them on mine. — I attracted his observation; he looked more eagerly at my face, and at last obliged me to retire, from a sentiment of modesty, which would not permit me to support so steady an observer. I, several days after this, saw the young man, who always paid me the same attention; but the garden was too closely guarded to permit him to speak, had he wished it.

One evening, as the refulgent radiance, with which the moon shone through my little grated casement, invited me to open it, while the recollection of those rural pleasures I had been accustomed to enjoy before my captivity; the charming scenes of variegated nature, which I remembered with peculiar delight, mixed with melancholy at the thoughts of enjoying them no longer, at last, imperceptibly introduced my dear departed mother to my mind, with many tender scenes of my childhood and youth, when I was the object of all her cares. — I know not how long I was engaged in these reveries, but that I was recalled from them by the well-known voice in the garden, who sung to his guitar the following words:

> I.
> How sweet the rose — the lilly fair,
> The morn of spring serene;
> How sweet the summer's closing day,
> And moonlight's silver scene.

> II.
> But sweeter far the gen'rous heart,
> With friendship's flame imprest;
> Or the first dawn of tender love,
> Which fires the artless breast.

III.
But where are nature's pleasing powers,
While darkness spreads its gloom?
And distant from the fragrant flowers,
We lose the sweet perfume.

IV.
Thus when the night of absence reigns,
The joys of converse shed;
Fair friendship droops, and plaintive strains,
Declare all pleasure dead.

I looked out with caution, lest he should observe my curiosity; but finding his eyes fixed on the window, I hastily withdrew myself; he then sung and played another air, expressive of love, and regret for the loss of liberty.

I shut the window hastily, and retired to my bed; but it was only to ruminate over this incident, in which I felt an excess of pain and pleasure. — Greatly rejoiced was I to be assured that this young man was the same person, whose sentiments and employments I was so well acquainted with. Pleased and captivated with his person also, I felt inexpressible delight, that I was not indifferent to him; but when I considered the situation we were both in, my sorrow was without bounds. — I spent the night in tears; and my passions, ever impetuous, were a source of misery to me, which found no relief from hope.

The next day, however, I resolved to improve the liberty I had of walking in the same garden, and which I had never an inclination to do before. I went out, and saw the young man at the window, who seemed delighted to see me there; at the next turn I saw him not, but was resolved to take another, in hopes of his returning again; he had retired to write the following billet, which he dropped at my feet. — I looked round, and seeing no one, took it up, and retired with it to my apartment.

An unfortunate man, who has been a prisoner of state more than six years; a stranger to joy; an alien from society, has received from the fair one this is addressed to, a delight unfelt before. Innocent of any crime, yet without any present prospect of a release, let your pity soften my solitude. — Let me have the pleasure of seeing you daily in this garden, and from this let me judge of your compassion.

Courtney.

This note afforded me exquisite delight: I found that this stranger had made an impression on my heart, which nothing could erase.

I waited with impatience the next day for the hour of walking; our eyes met, and easily explained to each other that our love was mutual. From this time, frequent letters to each other imparted our sentiments, while I continued to be the invisible and silent auditor of his solitary amusements: which I was resolved, however, not to inform him of; as I thought it would set him on his guard more, and I should not be enabled to judge so well of the sincerity of his love for me, which I did not doubt would influence his amusements; in this I was not deceived, for instead of learned studies, almost all his attention was now constantly turned to subjects of poetry and sentiment. — Almost every day produced new compositions of his own, on those themes; but the despair which ran through them, awoke my tenderest compassion.

One day, when I was walking in a retired part of the garden, I was surprised to see Courtney hastening to meet me; — as soon as he approached, he said his love and despair had determined him to risk every thing, for the pleasure of a moment's conversation with me; that it was against the rules of the place, for more than one prisoner to be in the garden at once, but that he had got down unobserved by the guard, though he knew he had not a moment to stay. — He then, in lively terms, expressed his passion; entreated me, if ever we were at liberty, to consent to be his; to inform him of my name and abode, and during our captivity, to answer his letters.

My solicitude for his safety, banished all reserve from my words and behaviour; I acknowledged my interest in his safety, and told him, I would inform him by a letter who I was, and any thing else he wished to know, earnestly beseeching him to be gone that instant. He threw himself at my feet, and kissed my hand, in an extacy of gratitude at my condescension, and hastily left me.

The next day I fulfilled my promise, and writ to him, acquainted him with my story, and the little hopes I had of obtaining my liberty; still concealing my knowledge of his solitary employments, but declaring myself so sincerely attached to him, that I did not wish for liberty while he continued a prisoner; recommending it to him, to hope that heaven would not permit us, innocent as we were of any crime against the state, to remain for ever in captivity; and adding, that patience and resignation were the most probable means of lightening, as well as shortening it. I threw this letter out at the window, and saw him take it up.

The next day, I went into the garden as usual, and walked some time, seeing him at the window; he left it, and I withdrew to the retired part of the garden, where I had before seen him, and determined to wait there till he had time to write, which I imagined he had gone away to do, when how was I shocked and surprised, to see him hastening to meet me! knowing, as I did, the danger of it; but I could not persuade him to leave me for nearly half an hour, nor would he permit me to leave him; at length, however, he went away, but he had been observed, and was reprimanded by the keeper severely, though respectfully, and suffered to go into his apartment.

I was soon after returning to mine, but was told, that our connection was discovered; first, by our communication by letters thrown out at the window, and then, by our interview in the garden; that it was an affair by no means to be permitted, and that, therefore, I must retire to another part of the Tower. The keeper then conducted me into the apartment that my poor mother died in, making an apology for his conduct, and saying he must fulfill his orders.

I was so struck with grief and horror at the place I was returned to, that it stopped my utterance, and suspended, at first, every other thought: all the circumstances of my mother's death recurred to my memory, and filled me with the keenest anguish. When I had exhausted those first emotions, I revolved in my mind my distance from Courtney, and the loss, perhaps, for ever, of his society. What a distracting idea! though my feelings were naturally violent, reason and virtue had always some power over them: no reason now came to my aid; even the dictates of religion were unattended to. The passion I felt for Courtney, the despair that the loss of his conversation possessed me with, unsoftened by any friendly remonstrances, undivested by any amusement of avocation, found within my breast a misery too great for any weak frame to support.

A violent fever succeeded the first distraction of my mind; I had every assistance afforded me, and a careful nurse to attend me; but for a long time I was insensible to every thing, and when my body was tolerably restored, a deep melancholy, and perfect indifference to life succeeded. I should not have attended to the food necessary for my existence, had not my nurse used every argument to prevail on me to eat of what they brought, which, to avoid being teized, I did.

At last, I was permitted to walk upon the battlements of the Tower for a little air, but not to go into the garden I used to frequent: my nurse supported my feeble steps, but as I could not walk far, I sat down disconsolately, mourning my hard fate; to be thus removed from the only person in the world who was interested about me, or who felt for me the sweet sentiments of friendship. Yet I, everyday, took the advantage they gave me of quitting my hated cell for a short time, thought a little fresh air was all the benefit I reaped from it, for I neither saw, nor heard, any thing of the unfortunate Courtney. This was my situation on your Majesty's entrance into the Tower, and on your enquiring what prisoners of rank were here, I was brought into your presence.

***

The fair Laurana here concluded her narrative: the Queen expressed the warmest esteem for her, said she should rejoice to give liberty of person and conscience to all, and to reign over a free people, whom she wished to attach to her, only by her solicitude to render them happy.

She added, that she feared so powerful a Duke as Norfolk, would not be permitted by her council to be set at liberty, and it would be too glaring a partiality to release Courtney without him, till her accession to the crown was a little more ratified by the voice of the people; that Mary was in arms, and the consent doubtful, but that however it terminated, it could not but be favorable to Courtney, and consequently to herself; she therefore entreated her to render herself completely easy, and be assured that they would be permitted to see each other as often as they pleased. She said, she would immediately send again for Courtney, who doubtless was very desirous to entertain his fair mistress.

A messenger was then sent for him, and he soon appeared, with that elegant and noble air, which is the effect of refined sentiments and a great mind. — That sickly languor, which was diffused over his face at his first entrance, was changed to a lively red, at the sight of the fair Lady Laurana.

The Queen, in the most animated terms, expressed her concern, that so amiable a young nobleman should have been so long secluded from society, to which he would have been as ornament. She said, she had frequently regretted his fate, during the life of

67

the late King, as his majesty also had; but he could not prevail on the Protector to release him. She then added the reasons before given to Lady Laurana which obliged her to detain him a little while longer in the Tower; but said, she would contribute all in her power to prevent his feeling himself a prisoner.

Courtney thanked her, with an appearance of ingenuous gratitude, for her goodness to him; and then approaching the object of his tenderest concern, who looked ready to faint, in the most affecting manner, he expressed his joy to see her again, whom he thought he had lost for ever; and a scene of tenderness passed between them, which I can never do justice to; and, indeed, we soon left them, thinking it would be more pleasing to them to enjoy their transports alone.

I afterwards required him to relate what his situation was, when he found he had lost his fair mistress. — He said, he had no intimation given him of Lady Laurana's departure from her room; he therefore watched all the next day for her appearance in the garden, and finding, toward dusk, that she did not come down as usual, he went into it himself, waiting for her appearance at her window, but she appeared not; he then played some of his favorite airs, and sung them to his guitar; still, however, no Laurana appeared, not even for a moment: as the darkest [fear of the worst] approached, he entreated her, in the most plaintive manner, to give him some signal of her being still in her room; but all in vain, no signal, no answering voice, no Laurana appeared.

Sometimes he thought she was dead; sometimes that she had left the Tower, and that he should never see her again; at other times, his gloomy mind, half-distracted with a horrid suspense, would imagine he heard her voice in screams of agony; he would then start from his bed, and listen with the most fearful attention; when every hollow step, every resounding echo, which broke through the silence of the night, in that mansion of strength, would raise a thousand dreadful ideas, and apparitions of horror to his distempered fancy.

At length time, that soother of grief, a little abated his distraction, and reason assumed, by slow degrees, her power over his soul, which enabled him to have recourse to his studies, and, after a while, allowed him to amuse himself with his guitar.

Though he avoided the subject of love with the greatest industry, he said he one day, without consideration, touched the notes of a little air, with which he first addressed Lady Laurana, on the subject of love. The words recurred to his memory, and, with them, the whole train of those ideas, which had almost deprived him of reason — the effect had almost again deranged his mind, and it was some days before he could recover any thing like tranquility.

This was his situation when the Queen's message reached him: he started from his seat, looked wildly round him, but could not, for a while, comprehend what was meaned by it.

So many events, new and astonishing to a man, who had been a prisoner more than six years, and, in all that time, and never known the least circumstance of what was doing in the world, only that Henry was dead, and succeeded by Edward, a minor, which he had learned from Lady Laurana's story. To be informed, at present, that Edward was also dead; that he had excluded his sister from the succession, and left his Crown to Lady Jane Grey, and that this new Queen had sent for him; what could it mean? to what new fate was he reserved!

Yet he reflected — I may, perhaps, see again my charming Laurana, if she still lives. This hope animated him to appear before the new Queen with some degree of resolution.

Both the Queen and myself were greatly affected, with the sufferings of these amiable lovers, and we shall rejoice exceedingly to see them happy.

Lady Laurana, and myself, are already united in a sincere and tender friendship. I know but of one fault she has, which is a little to much bigotry to the religion she has been brought up in, by which I do not mean constancy, which I approve of as much as she does, but want of charity.

But all her passions and feelings are naturally violent and excessive; yet her manners are gentle, and her heart artless and good, and she takes infinite pains to preserve the authority of reason over her soul. She is a charming woman, and, as her health returns, those beauteous eyes, over which sickness had cast her veil, now shine every day with increasing splendour, as do also her lover's, who is one of the finest figures, and has the most animated countenance I ever saw.

I have written you a long letter, my Catherine. Inform me very soon that your health is amended, which I am exceedingly sorry to hear is so interrupted; and that you will come and pay your duty to your Queen, who has now a claim to your attention superior to that of sister.

Adieu, my dearest cousin,

Your Anne Grey [Lane 114].

The story in that letter is material for a novel of romance. Because of the sensitive nature of the imprisonment of Edward Courtenay and Lady Laurana, a review of their cases was postponed until such time as Jane had been on the throne a while and things in general had settled down.

Meanwhile, Guildford attended meetings of Council, a body so cowed by the bluster of royalty that the Duke of Northumberland made most decisions. Jane signed papers as they were put before her.

On July 11, Queen Jane wrote to the Marquess of Northampton, Lord Lieutenant of Surrey, Northampton, Bedford and Berks, asserting her possession of the kingdom and requiring his allegiance and defense of her title. This letter was composed under the direction of the Duke of Northumberland and the Duke of Suffolk.

> Jane the Queen,
> Right trusty and right well beloved Cousin, we greet you well, advertising the same that where yet hath pleased Almighty God to call to his mercy out of this life our dearest Cousin the King your late sovereign Lord, by reason whereof and such Ordinances as the said late King did establish in his life time for the security and wealth of this Realm, we are entered into our rightful possession of this Kingdom, as by the last Will of our said dearest Cousin, our late progenitor, and other several instruments to that effect signed with his own hand and sealed with the great Seal of this Realm in his own presence, whereunto the Nobles of this realm for the most part and all our Council and Judges, with the Mayor and Aldermen of our City of London, and divers other grave personages of this our Realm of England, have also subscribed there names, as by the same Will and Instrument it may more evidently and plainly appear; We therefore do You to understand, that by the ordinance and sufferance of the heavenly Lord and King, and by the assent and consent of our said Nobles and Counselors, and others before specified, We do this day make our entry into the Tower of London as rightful Queen of this Realm; and have accordingly set further our proclamations to all our loving subjects giving them thereby to understand their duties and allegiance which they now of right owe unto us as more amply by same you shall briefly per-

ceive and understand; nothing doubting, right trusty and right well beloved cousin, but that you will endeavor yourself in all things to the uttermost of your power, not only to defend our just title, but also assist us in our rightful possession of this kingdom, and to disturb, repel, and resist the fained and untrue claim of the Lady Mary bastard daughter to our great uncle Henry the Eighth of famous memory; wherein as you shall do that which to your honor, truth, and duty appertained, so shall we remember the same unto you and yours accordingly. And our further pleasure is that you shall continue, do, and execute every thing and things as our Lieutenant within all places, according to the tenor of the Commission addressed unto you from our late Cousin King Edward the VI in such and like sort as if the same had been, as we mind shortly it shall be, renewed, and by us confirmed under our great Seal unto you.

Given under our Signet at our Tower of London the xi[th] of July, the first year of our Reign.

To our right trusty and right well beloved Cousin and Counsellor the Marques of Northampton our Lieutenant general of our County of Surrey and to our trusty and well beloved the Deputies of that Lieutenancy, and the Sheriff, the chief of Justices of Peace and the worshipful of that Shire [Ellis 183].

Another letter, undated and believed by some to be from July also, was also the work of Northumberland and Suffolk. Addressed to the Commissioners in Flanders, it requests that several items be brought to the attention of the emperor, including the death of Edward VI and the accession of Lady Jane as queen. The letter indicates that Northumberland's kinsman, Henry Dudley, carried the letter from the Council to the commissioners.

After our hearty commendations you shall perceive by the bearer, Mr. Shelley, and by such letters as you shall receive from the Queens Highness our Sovereign Lady Queen Jane, with copy of such Letters as her Grace send to the Emperor, what is the cause of this message now sent to you, and what it is that [is] now to be done by you there: first, the signification of our Sovereign Lords death; next, the possession of the Queens Highness in the Crown of this Realm; thirdly, the placing of you, Sir Phillip Hoby, Knight, as Ambassador there resident; fourthly and last, the offer for your remaining there to proceed in the Treaty of the Peace, if it shall so like the Emperor. Furthermore, ye shall understand that although the Lady Mary, hath been written unto from us to remain quiet, yet never the less we see her not so way the matter, that if she might she would disturb the state of this Realm, having thereunto as yet no manner appearance of help or comfort, but only the concurrence of a few lewd, base people; all other the nobility and gentlemen remaining in their duties to our Sovereign Lady Queen Jane. And yet never the less because the conditions of the baser sort of people is understood to be unruly if they be not governed and kept in order, therefore for the meeting with all events, the Duke of Northumberland's Grace, accompanied with the Lord Marquess of Northampton, proceed with a convenient power into the parties of Norfolk to keep those countries in stay and obedience; and because the Emperors Ambassadors here remaining shall in this matter of the policy not intermeddle, as it is very likely they will and do dispose themselves, the Lord Cobham and Sir John Mason repair to the same Ambassadors to give them notice of the Lady Mary's proceedings against the state of this Realm; and to put them in remembrance of the nature of their office, which is not to meddle in these causes of policy, neither directly nor indirectly; and so to charge them to use them selves as they give no occasion of unkindness to be ministered unto them, whereof we would be most sorry for the amity which one our party we mean to conserve and maintain. And for that percase the Ambassadors, and what the very message is, using it in such sort as thereby as the amity may best be preserved [Ellis, 1846 series, 310].

Many thought Mary should have succeeded Edward, not Lady Jane, and they swore allegiance to Mary and joined her.

By July 12, it was clear to Northumberland that military operations would be needed if he were to defeat the growing but still leaderless army of Mary at Kenninghall and capture the princess. Northumberland had other problems, as well. He was certainly the most accomplished military leader, but he did not trust the resolution of some of his colleagues and wanted to remain in London to protect his interests. The Duke of Suffolk could have led the forces, but Jane refused to send her father into battle. She feared being left alone with the duke; so Northumberland led the force himself. "In a few days I will bring the Lady Mary, captive, ordered like a rebel as she is," he said as he departed the Tower (Taylor 131).

The same day, a letter over the queen's signature to the ambassadors at Brussels directed Sir Philip Hoby to remain with the emperor and the other commissioners to stay and negotiate a peace treaty.

Trusty and Wel beloved, We greet you well. It hath so pleased God of his Providence, by calling of Our most dead Cousin of famous Memory, King Edward VI. out of this Life, to Our very natural Sorrow, that We, both by our said Cousin's lawful Determination in his Life-time, with the Assent of the nobility and States of this Realm, and also as the lawful Heir and Successor in the whole Blood Royal, are possessed of this Our Realm of England and Ireland: Wherefore, We have presently sent to Our good Brother, the Emperor, this present Bearer here, Our trusty Servant Mr. Richard Shelly, with Letters of Recommendations and Credence from Us; thereby signifying unto him, as well the sorrowful Death of Our said Cousin the King, as also Our Succession in the Crown of this realm: Motioning unto Our said good Brother the Continuance in such Amity and League, as Our said Cousin and Predecessor had with him. For which Purpose We have furthermore signified, by Our said Letters, not only Our Order, that you, Sir Philip Hoby, shall there remain and reside with Our good Brother the Emperor, as Our Ambassador Resident; praying you to give him Credit appertaining to such an Office; but also, that for the like Zeal and Desire We have to the Weal of Christendom, as our said Cousin King Edward had, wherein We do covet to follow his steps, We have given Order, that ye, the whole Number of Our Ambassadors, shall remain, to continue to proceed in the former Commission which ye had from Our Ancestor the King, if it shall please Our said good Brother. The Copy of which Our Letters We send to you herewith, for your more ample understanding of Our Determination; which considered and pondered, We would ye made your most speedy Access to Our said good Brother, in order to execute the Matters contained in the said Letters, on your Parts to be declared: First, The Signification of the Death of our said Ancestor and Cousin the King; whereof as We by Nature must take great Grief; so We doubt not but Our said good Brother will, for friendship and great Amity, sorrow and condole with Us: Next, That you Sir Philip Hoby have express Order there to reside, and attend upon Our good Brother as Our Minister, for the Continuance and Entertainment of the Intelligence and firm Amity, heretofore had and concluded between Our said Ancestor and Cousin the King, and Our said good Brother; the Maintenance whereof, We, with the Assent of Our Nobility and Council, do much desire; and for Our Parts will not fail, but confirm and maintain the same.

In the End you shall shew to Our said good Brother, That as We do, by God's providence, succeed to Our said Ancestor and Cousin King Edward, in this Our Crown and Dominion, so do We find in Our Heart and Mind, the very Descent and Inheritance of his most Christian Devotion and Affection to the Commonwealth of Christendom: Which moveth Us, with the Advice of Our Nobility and Council, to offer to Our said good Brother the Ministry and Office of you, Our Ambassadors, to remain there; and proceed in the former Commission, for the Conciliation of some good Peace between our said good Brother and the French King; wherein We refer our good Purpose and Meaning to the Mind and Contentation of Our said good Brother.

Thus done, whatsoever Our good Brother shall answer, ye may thereunto reply as ye think expedient, tending to the Continuance of Our Ancestor's Amity. For the rest of the Proceedings, ye shall understand by the Bearers: to whom We would ye should give Credit.

Given under Our Signet at Our Tower of London, the XII of July, 1553 [Strype 1721 edition, 5].

A letter dated July 12 from the Council to the sheriff and justices of peace of Nottinghamshire and Derbyshire requested their assistance.

After our most hearty commendations. Where as the Queens Highness Queen Jane, being presently by just title in full possession of the imperial crown of this realm and other dominions and p'hemynencs there unto belonging; the Lady Mary bastard daughter of the late King of famous memory King Henry the eighth doth not only by all the ways and means she may, stir and provoke the common people of the realm to rebellion, but also seeketh means to bring in great sorts of Papists Spaniards and other strangers for the aid of her unjust and unnatural pretence, to the great peril and danger of the utter subversion of God's holy word and of the whole state of this realm, we nothing doubt but these seditious and rebellious doings of the Lady Mary being well known unto you will of themselves well admonish you of your duties to yours and ours said loving Lady Queen Jane and preservation of the true religion and ancient liberty of your natural country against foreign powers: Yet considering what desolution may come to men of worship and good degree and wealth by the sedissions rebellions and montyones of the Bastards force; we have thought good to signify unto you that our said loving Lady Queen Jane's pleasure and commandment is that ye shall not only use all manner of travel and labor to keep and preserve her majesties people inhabiting near about you in peace and good guyett, and to repress all others that shall go about to move any tumult either by pretence of the unjust and feigned title of the Lady Mary being illegitimate and bastard as is aforesaid, or by any other means, but also to put your selves in order with such numbers of horsemen and footmen as you be able to make of your servants, tenants and others under your rules and offices, so as you may upon sending for, or further knowledge given you, either repair to our good lord the Duke of Northumberland, who having with him our very good Lord the Marquess of Northampton the Earl of Huntington and other personages of estate, is presently in the field with our said sovereigns power for the repression of the said rebellion, or other ways be employed for the defense of the realm, as the case shall require. By your good travel therein you shall not only declare your selves good and pay the full ministers to the Queens Highness and your country, but also will deserve to find her highness your good and gracious lady in any your reasonable suttees; and as also most ready to further your said suttees accordingly. And thus far[e] you most hearty well.

From the Tower of London the XIJ day of July 1553.

Your assured loving friends
T. Cant.Pembroke.
T. Ely, Canc.G. Cobham.
Winchester.Edward Northe.
F. Bedford.Jo. Mason.
F. Shrewsbury.Robert Bowes.

"To our loving friends the Sheriff of Nottingham and Derbyshire, and to the Justices of peace of the said countries and to every of them" [Nicolas 504].

Jane's decision not to send her father proved fatal to Northumberland's plans. The restraint that Northumberland had over the Council while in his presence was now gone and the lords began to establish who their allies were.

Reports of the size of Northumberland's forces vary from 1,500 to 8,000 foot soldiers, 2,000 horses, and a small train of artillery, but whatever their strength, on the morning of July 13 they departed. The Duke of Northumberland reportedly said to Lord Gray of Wilton, who accompanied him, "Do you see, my lord, what a conflux of people here is drawn to see us march? And yet of all this multitude, you hear not so much as one that wisheth us success" (Beer, *Rebellion & Riot*, 157).

On July 15, the Council while in London received a letter dated July 12 from Sir Philip Hoby and Sir Richard Morysine, commissioners, who where in Brussels.

> Please it your good Lordship's,
> The xiiij of this present, Don Diego found me, Sir Philip Hoby, and me Richard Morrison, walking in our Host's garden, and at his first coming to us, entered into a long talk, how much he was bound to owe his good will and service to England, and therefore he could not but at one time both sorrow with us for the loss of our old master, a Prince of such virtue and towardness, and also rejoice with us, that our master which is departed, did ere he went, provide us of a king, in whom we had so many causes to rejoice in, he made his excuses that [he] had not come to us the day before, laying the stay thereof in D. Arras; for saith he, when I told him I would come to you, and shew me a partaker both of your sorrows and gladness, with mind to make offer to the King's Majesty by you both, of as much service as should lye in me, and of as much as my friends and kinsmen were able to do, in case D. Arras did think such my offer could not offend the Emperor my master, D. Arras' advice was, that I should for a season defer my going unto you, which as I did somewhat against my will, so I am now very glad that I so did, for he telleth me now I may come to you, and sorrow with you, and make all the offers that I can to the King's Majesty, for I shall not only not offend him in so doing, but

I shall much please his Majesty therewith; and therefore saith he, as I am sorry that ye have lost so good a King, so do I much rejoice that ye have so noble and so toward a Prince to succeed him, and I promise you by the word of a gentleman, I will at all times serve his Highness myself, and as many as I shall be able to bring with me, if the Emperor did call me to serve him. We said, we hitherto had received the sorrowful news, but the glad tidings were as yet come unto us by no letters; we were glad to hear thus much, and wished that we were able to tell him all, how things went at home: saith he, I can tell you thus much. — The King's Majesty for dis-charge of his conscience, wrote a good piece of his Testament with his own hand, barring both his sisters of the Crown, and leaving it to the Lady Jane, niece to the French Queen. Whether the two daughters be base or no, or why it is done, we that be strangers have nothing to do with the matter; you are bound to serve and obey his Majesty, and therefore it is reason we take him for your King, whom the consent of the nobles of your country have allowed for your King. I, saith he, for my part of all others, am bound to be glad that his Majesty is settled in this office; I was his god-father, and will as willingly spend my blood in his service, as any subject that he hath, as long as I shall see the Emperor my master so willing to embrace his Majesty's amity. Don Francisco de Este, general of all the footmen Italians, is gone to his charge in Milan, who at his departure made the like offer, as long as his mas-ter and ours should be friends, which he trusted should be ever, praying us at our return to utter it to the King's Majesty, and thus we humbly take our leaves of your honors, from the Commission-ers at Brussels, the xv of July, 1553.

A short note follows, but its connection to the letter is doubtful.

> That it hath liked your Grace to promise to consider my suit, I most humbly thank you for hoping your goodness will at conve-nient leisure take a time to remember the same, and dispatch me (Nicholas 63).

Meanwhile, Mary moved her growing army from Kenninghall to Framlingham. Her advisers expected a major battle, and Kenninghall was not easily defensible. Men of substance were joining her ranks, but the great lords had not yet moved.

Rumors of desertions from Northumberland's ranks spread. A demand for replacements reached the Tower on the night of July 15.

A letter from the Council at the Tower went the same day to the sheriff and magistrates of Wiltshire, reaffirming Jane's claim to the crown and reporting Northumberland's intent to capture Mary. The letter's tone indicates the lack of cohesion among the lords of the Council.

> After our most hearty commendations: albeit it hath been heretofore openly published in all parts of this realm, by open proclamation, letters, and many other ways, upon what good grounds of nature, justice, and common order, our most gracious sovereign lady, Queen Jane, is presently invested, and in just possession of the imperial crown of this realm of England, France, and Ireland, with all authorities, right, and pertinencies thereunto belonging; yet forasmuch as the Lady Mary, bastard daughter of the noble Prince, King Henry the Eighth, seeking daily more and more, by all ways and means she can, to stir and move sundry of the nobles, gentlemen, and others, the Queen's Majesty's subjects to rebellion, ceaseth not to spread and set forth most traitorously sundry untrue reports of our sovereign Lady Queen Jane, and falsely also of some of us, of her Majesty's privy council, we have though[t] good, by these our letters, to open and declare unto you in few words, the very truth and original grounds of this matter, which is, that our late master and sovereign Lord, King Edward the Sixth, considering that if the crown imperial of this realm should have descended to his bastard sister, the said Lady Mary, it should have been prejudicial to all those that be of the whole blood, descended of the imperial crown of this realm, and been occasion of the utter disherison of all personages descended of the said blood royal; and a mean to the bringing in of strangers, whereof was like to have followed the bondage of this realm, the old servitude of the antichrist of Rome, the subversion of the new preaching of God's word, and of the ancient laws, usages, and liberties, did first in his life time will, declare, and limit the said imperial crown, to remain in such sort and order, as we and our posterities, by the grace of God, might be well assured to live many years, under princes naturally born in this realm, and lawfully begotten, and descending of the blood royal of the same. Unto which his pleasure being by himself, in his royal person,

openly declared unto us, long before his death, not only we and every of us, being of his Majesty's privy council, did consent and subscribe, but the most part of all the nobility of this realm, judges, the mayor and aldermen of London, and many other grave personages, of good reputation, did also subscribe and agree. According to which limitation and agreement of the state aforesaid, our said sovereign lady is presently in actual and real possession of the said imperial crown, not by any special procurement of particular men, but by the full consent and agreement of the whole state, as is aforesaid, whereunto as we did at the beginning with good deliberation asse[n]t and agree, upon many just and good grounds, so do we still wholly remain and, God willing, mind always to remain of that same concord, to maintain and defend to the death, our said sovereign lady Queen Jane's just title, during our lives. Sorry we be, that these unnatural seditions and tumults stirred by the said bastard, to the great danger of this realm, should in this sort disquiet you or any other of the Queen's Majesty's subjects, for the stay whereof it might have liked her, to have been contented with the honorable state she was by the noble prince King Henry the Eighth left in, and by our late sovereign lord and master King Edward the Sixth confirmed, and increased, nothing hath been on our behalf omitted. But, considering that by the counsel of a number of obstinate papists, she forsaketh, as by her seditious proclamations appears, the just title of supremacy, annexed to the imperial crown of this realm, and consequently to bring in again the miserable servitude of the Bishop of Rome, to the offence of Almighty God, and utter subversion of the whole state of this realm, the Queen's Majesty hath appointed our very good lord the Duke of Northumberland, and with him the Lord Marquis of Northampton, the Earl of Huntingdon, the Lord Admiral, and other noblemen, to go forward for the stay of the said seditions and tumults, whereof we have at good length made you privy by these our letters; so we doubt nothing, but considering your duties to Almighty God, your natural sovereign lady, Queen Jane, and your country, you will conform yourselves to the common tranquility of peace and concord of the nobility of this realm, travailing by all ways and means, that all occasions of rebellions and tumults, upon any pretence of the said bastard daughter's unlawfull claim or otherwise may be staid, and the authors or procurers of any such apprehended and punished; whereby you shall not only eschew the punishment of the laws, ordained for such as shall attempt any thing against their sovereign lord or lady, being in possession of the imperial crown; but also be well assured to find our said lady, Queen Jane, your good and gracious lady, and most willing to further any your most reasonable suits, when occasion shall serve; and so fare ye most heartily well.

From the Tower of London, the 15th day of July, anno 1553.

Signed, T Cant.; T. Eli Canc.; Winchest.; Bedford; Suffolk; Arundell; Shresbury; Pembroke; G. Cobham; R. Cotton; T. Cheyney; Jo. Mason; Robart Bowes [Hoare 266].

On the morning of July 16, the Duke of Northumberland reached the outskirts of Cambridge, and as he proceeded toward Bury St. Edmunds, news reached him from Yarmouth of the desertion of eight ships stationed there to seize the Princess Mary if she tried to escape overseas. The crew swore allegiance to Mary, yet another blow to the duke's plans.

The same day the queen sent notice to the sheriff, justices, and gentlemen of Surrey, admonishing them not to credit Mary's letters.

Jane the Queen.

Trusty and well beloved we greet you well. Albeit that our estate in this Imperial Crown whereof we be actually and really possessed, as partly may appear by our Proclamation, wherein our title is published, is not, nor can be any wise doubtful to all such our good faithful subjects, as setting blind affection apart, do in reason and wisdom consider the very foundation and ground of our title, with the great commodities thereby coming through God's providence to the preservation of our common weal and policy; yet for that we understand the Lady Mary doth not cease by Letters in her name, provoked thereto by her adherents, enemies of this Realm, to publish and notify slanderously to divers of our subjects matter derogatory to our title and dignity royal, with the slander of certain of our Nobility and Council: We have thought meet to admonish and exhort You, as our true and faithful subjects, to remain fast in your obeisance and duty to the Imperial Crown of this Realm, whereof we have justly the possession; and not to be removed any wise from your duty by slanderous reports or letters, dispersed abroad either by the said Lady Mary, or by her adherents; for truly like as the Nobility of our Realm, our Council, our Prelates, our Judges, and learned men, and others, good wise, godly and natural subjects, do remain fast and surely in their Allegiance towards us, ready to adventure their lives, lands, and goods for our defense, so can a great number of the same Nobility, Counsellors, and Judges, truly testify to all the world, with safety of their conscience, how carefully and earnestly the late King of famous memory, our dear Cousin King Edward the Sixth, from time to time mentioned and provoked them partly by persuasion, partly commandants, to have such respect to his succession, if God should call him to his mercy without issue, as might be the preservation of the Crown in the whole undefiled English Blood. And therefore of his own mere motion, both by grant of his Letters Patents, and by declaration of his will, established the successions as it is declared by our Proclamation. And for the testimony hereof to the satisfaction of such as shall conceive any doubt herein, We understand that certain of our Nobility have written to you at this present, in some part to admonish you of your duties, and to testify their knowledge of the truth of our title and right. Wherefore we leave to proceed further therein, being assured in the goodness of God, that your hearts shall be confirmed to owe your duty to us your Sovereign Lady, who mean to preserve this Crown of England in the royal blood, and out of the dominion of strangers and papists, with the defense of all you our good subjects, your lives, lands, and goods, in our peace against the invasions and violence of all foreign or inward enemies and rebels.

Given under our Signet at our Tower of London, xvj day of July, in the first year of our reign.

To our trusty and well beloved the Sheriff, Justices of Peace, and other Gentlemen of our County of Surry, and to every of them [Kempe 124].

On the night of July 16, news arrived that the Princess Mary had been proclaimed queen in Oxford. Lady Jane, still in residence in the state apartments in the Tower, found that the Earls of Pembroke and Winchester had left the Tower for their homes and quickly dispatched the guards to retrieve them. From that point onward, all the gates were locked and the keys brought to Queen Jane by seven o'clock every night.

On July 17, as the Duke of Northumberland retreated from Bury St. Edmunds to Cambridge, a letter from Sir Philip Hoby and Sir

Richard Morysone addressed to the Council arrived describing their audience the previous day with the emperor.

> To the Lords of the Council,
> Please it your good Lordships, the xvi of this month, we declared to the Emperor our heavy and sorrowful news, setting forth, after that your Lordship's assured good wills and readiness at all times to observe and maintain the ancient amity which had been always betwixt the realm of England and House of Burgundy, and other the Emperor's dominions, according to your Lordship's pleasures, signified to us in your letters of the ix day of this present month; for answer whereunto the Emperor said that he was right sorry for his part of these heavy news, whereby he perceived the loss of such a brother, and so good a friend both to him and to his countries, and considering that he was of such a great towardness, and of such hope to do good, and be a stay in Christendom, his loss was so much the greater; and used in this behalf many good words to our late Sovereign Lord's commendation and declarations of his grief for his death: and touching, saith he, the amity which hath been betwixt me and my late good brother, our countries and subjects, as I have always had good will to the observance of the same, according to such treaties as were betwixt us, so now understanding by you, my Lords of the Council's good inclinations, and minds to entertain and observe this amity for correspondency, I both now have and shall have like good will to keep and continue the same, and I thank them for making me understand their good will herein; with compliments of many other words to this purpose. So that as far as we can perceive by his words, he mindeth assuredly to keep amity with us, yet to decipher him better herein, it were not amiss in our opinions, when as your Lordship's shall advertise him, either with some new league or to tempt him what he will say to the old, or by some other means, which your wisdoms can better devise, &c.
> Dated the xvii July, 1553 [Nicolas 60].

That same day the guard at the Tower was doubled in the event of an uprising against Lady Jane. Reports arrived of Mary's increasing popularity and the hatred festering toward the Duke of Northumberland for not allowing her to claim what was hers.

Two letters the next day, July 18, indicated the desperation evident among Lady Jane's ever decreasing circle of followers. The first bears the queen's signature and is addressed to Sir John St. Lowe and Sir Anthony Kingstone, Knights, commissioning them to muster forces and march to Buckinghamshire to repress the rebellion as soon as possible. Rumors reported that Mary's forces were about 30,000, but there is no corroborating evidence, and the number seems unlikely.

> To our trusty and well beloved
> Sir John St. Lowe, and Sir
> Anthony Kingstone, Knts.

> JANE, the Queen
> Trusty and Well beloved, We greet you well. Because We doubt not, but by this our most lawful possession of the Crown, with the free Consent of the Nobility of our Realm, and other the States of the same, is both plainly known and accepted of you, as our most Loving Subjects, Therefore We do not reiterate the same. But now most earnestly Will Require, and by Authority hereof warrant you to assemble, muster, and levy all the Power that you can possible make, either of your Servants, Tenants, Officers, or Friends, as well Horsemen as Footmen, repairing to our Right Trusty and Right Well Beloved Cousins, the Earls of *Arundel* and *Pembroke*, their Tenants, Servants, and Officers and with the same to repair with all possible Speed towards *Buckinghamshire*, for the repressing and subduing of certain Tumults and Rebellions moved there against Us and Our Crown by certain seditious Men. For the repressing whereof, We have given Orders to divers others our good Subjects and Gentlemen of such Degree as you are, to repair in like Manner to the same Parts. So as We nothing doubt, but upon the Access of such our loving Subjects as be appointed for that Purpose to the Place where those seditious People yet remain, the same shall either lack Hearts to abide in their malicious Purpose, or else receive such Punishment and Execution as they deserve; seeking the Destruction of their native Country, and the Subversion of all Men in their Degrees, by Rebellion of the base Multitude: Whose Rage being stirred, as of late Years hath been seen, must needs be the Confusion of the whole Common weal.

Wherefore Our special Trust is in your Courage, Wisdom, and Fidelities in this matter, to advance yourselves both with Power and Speed, to this Enterprise, in such Sort as by our Nobility and Council shall be also prescribed unto you. And for the Sustentation of your Charge in this Behalf, our said Council, by our Commandment, do forthwith give Order to your Satisfaction, as by our Letters also shall appear unto you. And beside that, We do assure you of our special Consideration of this your Service to Us, our Crown, and especially to the Preservation of this our Realm and Commonwealth. Given under Our Signet at Our Tower of *London*, the xviii of *July*, in the first Year of our Reign [Strype Appendix II].

The second letter is very similar, though this one is addressed to Sir John Brydges and Sir Nicholas Poyntz. The British Library has affirmed that this document, presently housed in their facility, is one of the few surviving known to be from Jane's own pen. It bears the only known signature of the Lady Jane as queen.

JANE, the Queen

Trusty and Well beloved, We greet you well. Because We doubt not, but by this our most lawful possession of the Crown, with the free Consent of the Nobility of our Realm, and other the States of the same, is both plainly known and accepted of you, as our most Loving Subjects, Therefore We do not reiterate the same. But now most earnestly Will Require, and by Authority hereof warrant you to assemble, muster, and levy all the Power that you can possible make, either of your Servants, Tenants, Officers, or Friends, as well Horsemen as Footmen, (repairing to our Right Trusty and Right Well Beloved Cousins, the Earls of *Arundel* and *Pembroke*, their Tenants, Servants, and Officers) and with the same to repair with all possible Speed towards *Buckinghamshire*, for the repressing and subduing of certain Tumults and Rebellions moved there against Us and Our Crown by certain seditious Men. For the repressing whereof, We have given Orders to divers others our good Subjects and Gentlemen of such Degree as you are, to repair in like Manner to the same Parts. So as We nothing doubt, but upon the Access of such our loving Subjects as be appointed for that Purpose to the Place where those seditious People yet remain, the same shall either lack Hearts to abide in their malicious Purpose, or else receive such Punishment and Execution as they deserve; seeking the Destruction of their native Country, and the

Subversion of all Men in their Degrees, by Rebellion of the base Multitude: Whose Rage being stirred, as of late Years hath been seen, must needs be the Confusion of the whole Common weal.

Wherefore Our special Trust is in your Courage, Wisdom, and Fidelities in this matter, to advance yourselves both with Power and Speed, to this Enterprise, in such Sort as by our Nobility and Council shall be also prescribed unto you. And for the Sustentation of your Charge in this Behalf, our said Council, by our Commandment, do forthwith give Order to your Satisfaction, as by our Letters also shall appear unto you. And beside that, We do assure you of our special Consideration of this your Service to Us, our Crown, and especially to the Preservation of this our Realm and Commonwealth. Given under Our Signet at Our Tower of *London*, the xviii of *July*, in the first Year of our Reign [Harleian, Article 416].

In the left margin of the manuscript from which this letter had been transcribed, beside the names of Arundel and Pembroke, is the comment written in pen, "Tho these Earls at this time were plotting against her."

The desertions sapping Northumberland's ability to maneuver and fight, coupled with the fact that Mary's forces were increasing and loyalties were shifting from Jane to her, shook the confidence of those who were still loyal to Northumberland's cause. Fearing that when Mary took the throne they would be convicted of treason, they abandoned Northumberland at the first opportunity. By the time the duke reached Cambridge, he had lost about half his following. Though the duke lost a great many men to desertion, he lost none in battle — for no battle occurred.

Jane's council continued to splinter, and a number of councilors met at the Earl of Pembroke's residence with Pembroke and Arundel in attendance. They denounced Northumberland, saying he was a "blood thirsty tyrant and Mary had the best title to the crown" (Loades, 264).

The Mayor of London had requested, and it was agreed, that if the Duke of Northumberland did not immediately respond to their missive, Arundel would go to Cambridge and arrest the villain who had led so many against Mary.

The turmoil among those close to Lady Jane appears in a letter from Lady Anne Grey to Lady Catherine Herbert.

> Ah, my dearest Lady Catherine, we have most dreaded news to tell you! — the victorious Mary is almost at our gates — the Duke of Northumberland is taken — and all ranks of people are ready to acknowledge the sister of Edward as their only rightful Queen.
>
> May God support Lady Jane — support us all to sustain this fatal blow to all our hopes. The Duke and Duchess, and Lord Guildford are almost distracted with apprehension; but the excellent Jane preserves the same serenity of mind; endeavors to console her parents and husband, and possesses that only true dignity, which is the same in all events.
>
> Lady Jane Dudley is inconsolable for her father-in-law, and husband, who is with him. Poor Lady, how I pity her; she has scarce known any thing but tragic scenes in her family.
>
> But if Mary succeeds, and there is now but little reason to doubt that she will, we shall be involved in one common ruin; our families so large, connected by intermarriages, and unanimous in the present cause. — I almost fear this news will retard the recovery of your health, my Catherine, but I could not avoid giving it you, and you might, from common report, hear it represented worse, perhaps, if possible, than it is.
>
> Lady Jane has prevailed on Lady Laurana, with great difficulty, and with the assistance of her lover's arguments, to retire into France or Italy, and remain in a convent till his release; and has appointed a person, whom she could confide in, to conduct her there in safety; but no words can do justice to their pathetic parting scene. — Surely, never were souls more formed for each other, nor more deeply impressed with that gift of heavenly sensibility; a gift which none would part with who possess it; and few, I believe, desire it, who do not; and which is, perhaps, more allied to misery than to happiness.
>
> In Lady Jane, indeed, her large share of it appears with high luster; being attempered with strength of reason, guarded by the balmy power of religion, which heals the wounds made by it before they rankle.

Farewell, dear Lady Catherine, may heaven prepare your mind to support every vicissitude; and, O that Lady Jane's party may yet be victorious.

Anne Grey [Lane 160].

A temporary resolution within the Council figures in a letter dated July 19 from Jane's Council to Lord Rich, the Lord Lieutenant of Essex, informing him of the treachery of the Earl of Oxford who had gone over to Mary. Pembroke and Arundel signed the letter, notwithstanding their denunciation of Northumberland.

After our right hearty commendations to your Lp. Although the matter contained in your letters of the Earl of Oxfords departing to the Lady Mary, be grievous unto us for divers respects, yet we must neads give your Lp. our hearty thanks for your ready advertisement thereof. Requiring your Lp. nevertheless like a Noble man to remain in that promise and steadfastness to our Sovereign Lady Queen Jane's service, as you shall find us ready and firm with all our force to the same. Which neither with honor, nor with safety, nor yet with duty we may now forsake.

From the Tower of London, the xixth of July, 1553.

T. Cant.T.Ely, Canc.Winchester.J. Bedford.

J. SuffolkArundel.F. Shrewsbury.

Pembroke.T. Darcy.Richard Cotton.

William Paget.T. Cheyne.Jo. Cheke.

W. Petre S.Robert Bowes.

Jo. Baker.

[Cranmer 164].

The council proclaimed Mary queen the same day, and the Council changed its allegiance publicly and officially by sending two of their number to tell Suffolk that Jane's reign was over; informing the foreign ambassadors that the Lady Mary was Queen; proclaiming Mary in London and the provinces; and sending her their loyal submission.

CHAPTER 3. POST-REIGN PERIOD

When the Duke of Suffolk learned that the game was up and his daughter's reign was ended, he went to her and forbade her further use of royal ceremonies and counseled her to be content with her return to private life. She replied calmly:

> Sir, I better brook this message, than my forced advancement to royalty; out of obedience to you and my mother I have grievously sinned, and offered violence to myself: now I do willingly, and as obeying the motions of my soul, relinquish the crown, and endeavor to salve those faults committed by others, if at least so great an error may be salved by a willing relinquishment and ingenuous acknowledgement [Beer, Riot & Rebellion, 160].

The following day, the Duke of Northumberland learned at Cambridge that Mary was proclaimed queen. At about five o'clock that evening he also proclaimed Mary at the Market-Cross in town, by throwing up his cap, among others, in token of joy. Within an hour he received the following letter in the name of Queen Mary, ordering him and his band to disarm.

> Ye shall command and charge in the Queen's Highness's Name, the said Duke to disarm himself, and to cease all his Men of War,

and to suffer no Part of his Army to do any Thing contrary to Peace, and himself to forbear Coming to this City, until the Queen's Pleasure be expressly declared unto him. And if he will shew himself like a good quiet Subject, we shall then continue, as we have begun, as humble Suitors to our Sovereign Lady the Queen's Highness for him, and his, as for ourselves. And if he do not, we will not fail to spend our Lives, in Subduing him and his. Item, ye shall declare the like Matter to the Marquis of Northampton, and all other Noblemen and Gentlemen, and to all Men with any of them. And ye shall, in all Places where you come, notify it, if the Duke of Northumberland do not submit himself to the Queen's Highness, Queen Mary, he shall be accepted as a Traitor. And all we of the Nobility, that were Counsellors to the late King, will, to the uttermost Portion, persecute him, and his, to their utter Confusion.

> Signed by *Thomas* Archbishop of *Canterbury*, *Thomas* Bishop of *Ely*, Chancellor; *William* Marquis of *Winchester*, Treasurer; *Henry* Duke of *Suffolk*; the Earls of *Bedford*, *Shrewsbury*, and *Pembroke*; *Thomas Darcy* Lord Chamberlain, *W. Peter* Secretary, *W. Cecil* 2nd Secretary, with others of the Council [Collins 24].

The reign of Lady Jane has been called an "unpleasant but trivial delay to the good times which were coming with the Queen everyone loved" (Chapman, *Lady Jane Grey*, 145).

Little information exists to indicate the state of Jane's mind. Probably she was frightened, upset and confused, but apparently she also felt relief. Lady Jane wrote to her sister Lady Catherine sometime between July 20 and the last week of July. The letter provides at least some insight to her mental and emotional state.

> The idle pageantry of state is over, my dear Catherine, and your sister, that upstart Queen, whom a fatal ambition has imposed on the people, is now, after a ten day's reign, deposed, and obliged to open her gates to the rightful successor.
>
> Mary is received by all; Papists and Protestants, all acknowledge her lawful Queen; she promises fair: may it please the Almighty, that the purity of our holy faith remain unaltered, and I shall rejoice at the change. — With regard to myself, I resigned my crown with that transcendent delight, which no words can

express; may I again be permitted to taste the joys of domestic life, they will be doubly cherished by me, from the short experience I have had of the toils of greatness, and the dangers of ambition; but I do not imagine we shall soon enjoy again our liberty. We are, indeed, permitted to converse with each other, which softens, in a great degree, our confinement. Yet I fear greatly for my friends; Northumberland's spirit is too well known, to imagine he will be secure from the Queen's resentment, and we have all but too much reason to fear lest we should not be spared.

May we be resigned to our fate; all is permitted by divine Providence, for wise purposes to us unknown. — Yet I greatly condemn myself, that I did not more obstinately resist their importunities, but that, with my eyes open to the precipice before me, I was so irresistibly biased by filial duty, as to plunge headlong over it, and bear down in my fall, so many of those that are dearest to me. — My folly is indeed unpardonable.

I am almost afraid to send this letter, yet there is in it nothing inimical to the Queen. I will commit it to Lady Anne's care, who has conveyed to you the others.

Adieu, do not grieve too much, my sweet sister; but endeavor to raise your mind above human events, and, with a stedfast soul, look to that scene of future happiness prepared for the virtuous. — I freely acknowledge my errors, yet has my heart never deviated from that rectitude of intention, which has been its solace through all the afflictions I have hitherto sustained, and will, I trust, support it at that closing hour, whenever it shall happen, when all mortal supports fail, and the feeble lamp of vitality is quivering on a point, and just about to take its flight for ever.

Pray for your

Jane Grey [Lane 165].

When, in the second paragraph, she says, "We are permitted to converse," one may speculate that she means Guildford. Comforting, indeed, to be able to communicate with the loved one(s) of whose downfall she was the vehicle! Did they feel a commensurate grief for having impelled her to it?

The Duke of Northumberland and his party surrendered at Cambridge to the Earl of Arundel on July 24. They reached London the following day at dusk to find large crowds lining the streets. The guards escorting the duke dealt severely with the mob which threw stones, rotten eggs, and filth from the gutters. One witness says that a dead cat was hurled at the duke. The mob made several attempts to rush him, shouting, "Death! Death to the traitor!" (Chapman 150). The once confident, powerful, and arrogant Duke of Northumberland was at last humbled.

The Tower now housed the duke, most of his family, and several who had been brought in with him. The following day, the Duke of Suffolk, among others, joined the growing list of prisoners. Jane and Guildford were arrested, with the Duchess of Northumberland, as early as July 23.

Suffolk then appears to have gained his freedom, on about July 31, with the understanding that he would surrender himself, if required to do so, at any time.

Within the first few days of August, Lady Jane composed a letter to Mary in an attempt to explain the events that led her to the throne. The following letter has been translated from its original 1594 Italian text by Steve Spalding from the University of Michigan. This letter may only exist in this form; it is the only known or surviving copy of the original drafted by Jane. The author has discovered no reference to the original letter and only one reference to the translated letter made by an early historian.

Letter from Lady Jane, who had already been proclaimed Queen, addressed to H. M. (Her Majesty) in the month of August of the year 1553, as she was in the Tower prison; or, reasoning made to the people, as she was about to die, to justify the misdeed she had been accused of on February 12, 1554.

Even if my guilt is such that without the queen's benignity and clemency I would have absolutely no hope of finding forgiveness nor asking for remission, I nevertheless place myself in God's hands, as I now know and confess my lack of prudence, for which I deserve a severe punishment. For I listened to those who, at that time, seemed wise not only to me but also to a great part of this Kingdom, and who now, to my detriment and theirs, and to the shame and blame of everyone, made known, with such a shameless audacity, the blameworthy and degrading deed that they had given someone what was not hers. I should not have accepted it (for which I blush and feel a just and reasonable shame to ask forgiveness for such a crime). I know that and without Her Majesty's tremendous mercy and infinite clemency and without it being known that I am not entirely responsible for the mistake I am accused of, there would not be a lot of reasons for me to conceive any hope. Therefore, however great my guilt is — and I acknowledge it — I was nevertheless charged and found guilty to an extent greater than the one I deserved. Even though it turned out that I took upon me that which I was not worthy of, nobody will ever be able to say that I either accepted or felt satisfied with it. At the time when it had publicly been said that there was no hope left for the King, the Duchess of Northumberland had already promised that I would stay home with my mother. However, her husband, who was the first one to tell me about the King, gave her to understand this shortly after. Consequently, after that she did not want me to leave home anymore, saying that if God wanted to call the King up unto His Mercy, for whose life there was nothing to be hoped anymore, I should go to the Tower immediately, as the King had made me the heir of his extended Kingdom. These unexpected words caused an alteration in me and upset my soul. Later, they even worsened my condition. But I did not give too much credit to these words and nevertheless went to my mother's. Because of that, the Duchess of Northumberland fell out with me, and together with the Duchess my mother, saying that if she had resolved to have me stay in her house, she would also have had her dear son, my husband, stay close to her. She told me she thought I would go to my husband's at any cost, and added that she would forever be offended by my behavior. In reality, I stayed at her place for a couple of nights, but eventually, I besought the favor of being allowed to go to Chelsea for my pleasure. I fell sick little after I got there, the Council sent for me and gave me to understand that I had to leave for Syon on that very night, in order to receive what the King ordered I should receive.

And the woman who brought me this piece of news was Lady Seymour [*Signora Sedmei*, in the Italian version], my sister-in-law and the daughter of the Duke of Northumberland, who told with a gravity greater than usual that it was necessary that I should go there, as indeed I did.

But once we got there, there was no one to be found, apart from the Duke of Northumberland, the Marquess of Northampton, the Earl of Huntington, the Earl of Arundel and the Earl of

Pembroke, who arrived there shortly after. They entertained me lavishly, before revealing to me that the King had died. I was entertained especially by the Earl of Huntington and the Earl of Pembroke, who, with unusual caresses and pleasantness, showed a great reverence toward me and my state, which was not appropriate. They got down on their knees and, in many other fashions, pretended to revere me. Acknowledging me as their superior lady (because of this, I felt infinitely confused and ashamed), they eventually had my mother, the Duchess Frances, the Duchess of Northumberland and the Marchioness of Northampton come where I was. As president of the Council, The Duke of Northumberland announced the death of King Edward, then he expounded all the reasons we had to celebrate the virtuous and commendable life King led and the excellent death he just had. Besides, he appeared to comfort himself and the others by greatly praising the prudence and the goodness The King showed for the Kingdom as well as the excellent care he took of it toward the end of his life, when he prayed God that He should defend [against] the Papal faith and free him from the government of his bad sisters. Then, he said that His Majesty had indeed considered an act of Parliament, where it had already been deliberated that whoever should acknowledge and accept the Most Serene Mary, that is the most serene M.V. (Italian: M.V.) or Elizabeth as heir to the English crown, should be held as traitor, as one of them had already proved disobedient to her Father, Henry VIII, and also to him regarding the truth of Religion. He added that they were enemies of the word of God and both bastard children. Thence, the King did not want them to become heirs to the Crown in any way, as he could disinherit them in any manner he wanted. Therefore, he ordered the Council before he died, that, for the honor we owed him, the love we had for Kingdom and the charity one owes to the Fatherland, we should obey his will. The Duke then added that I was the one nominated by His Majesty to succeed him, and that my sisters should similarly succeed me, in the case of a breach of my seed. These words said, all the Lords of the Council fell down on their knees and told me that they would honor me in the way that suited my person, because I was the one who was of true and direct descent and heir to this Crown. They added that it was their duty to respect this in the best way possible, as they had promised the King, risking their lives and making blood flow if needed. As soon as I got to understand these words, my soul suffered infinitely — I will leave the Lords who were present at that time bear witness to my being utterly dazed and dejected: suddenly and unexpectedly, I was overcome by a great suffering, and the Lords saw me fall on the floor and weep with great distress. I announced my being unworthy for such a role and I deeply regretted the death of such a noble Prince. I turned to God, I humbly prayed and besought him that he would make it so that what had just been given to me was rightfully and legitimately mine. I also prayed that His Late Majesty should give me grace of spirit, so that I could govern this Kingdom in praise of him and prove serviceable to it. Later on the following day (as everyone knows), I was brought to the Tower and the Marquess of Winchester, the great Treasurer, gave me the jewels and together with them, he also brought the Crown. It so happened that, without my asking him or others asking him in my name, he wanted me to put the Crown on my head, to see if it fitted or not. I refused to do it, resorting to a number of excuses, but he added that I should be brave and take it, and also that he would make another to crown my husband. I listened to these words with a discomforted and reluctant spirit, and an infinitely displeased heart. After the above mentioned Lord left, I discussed a lot of things with my husband, and he agreed to being crowned King, and that he would have me do it with an act of Parliament, But then, I called the Earl of Arundel and the Earl of Pembroke and told them that I would be happy to make my husband a duke, and that I would never agree to his becoming King. His mother learnt about my resolution (my thought had been reported to her), which made her burst into a great anger and disdain. Her getting badly angry and scornful with me convinced her son that he should not sleep with me any longer, and so he did. He also told me that he had absolutely no desire to become either Duke or King. Thence, I was forced to send him the Earl of Arundel and the Earl of Pembroke. They tried to negotiate with him and make it so that he would come unto me, because I knew that otherwise, he would have gone to Syon. And this is the way in which I was fooled by the Duke, the Council as well as my husband, and was ill-treated by his mother. Besides, as [Lord/knight John (Dudley?)] *cavalier Giangatto* confessed, he was the first one to persuade King Edward to name me as heir. In the meantime, I do not know what the Council had determine[d] to do, but I know for sure that at that time, I was poisoned twice. The first time was in the house of the Duchess of Northumberland and the second, in the Tower, for which I have excellent and reliable witnesses. Besides, from that time on, all my hairs have fallen off my body. All these things I wanted to say, to bear witness to my innocence and relieve my conscience. [Facciotti 355]

In a very colorful trial, the Duke of Northumberland was convicted of high treason and sentenced to death on August 23, the execution to be carried out on Tower Hill. The "lame" headsman competently dispatched him with a single blow. He was buried in the chapel of St. Peter-ad-Vincula above Anne Boleyn and Katherine Howard and next to Somerset. A short work, "The saying of John late Duke of Northumberland upon the scaffold," was published immediately after the execution.

A letter from Lady Anne to Lady Laurana, by then settled in a convent in Florence, painted a vivid picture of the events after Mary seized the throne from Lady Jane. Written the last two weeks of August, the letter mentions the Duke of Northumberland's execution on August 23 as well as Mary's review of the prisoners in the Tower on August 3. The new queen created Edward Courtenay Earl of Devonshire soon thereafter.

> You have, perhaps, by public report, my friend, heard that Lady Jane is deposed, and Mary acknowledged Queen of England.
> Your friendly heart will feel for our distress, and the ill-success of that excellent Lady, who yet would return to private life, with the highest satisfaction, might she hope that Mary's fears would permit her consideration of her as no consequence. She has, indeed, professed to pardon both Lady Jane and her Lord, as well as the Duke of Suffolk; but I distress much that it will be revoked again, as they are not permitted to quit the Tower.
> The Duke of Northumberland has suffered for his ambition, and with him two others, who were principals in the party, but no others nearly related to us.
> The Queen's lenity has gained her great popularity, in punishing no more on this occasion.
> Lord Guildford, who was possessed of the highest filial affection, morns incessantly for his father's violent death, and his affectionate wife shares his grief — they are actuated but by one soul — and it is impossible for either to feel a sorrow, which the other partakes not of.

96

As soon as Mary arrived at the gates of the Tower, the Duke of Suffolk immediately opened them to her, and was the first to acknowledge her his rightful Sovereign. Mortifying, indeed, was this to him, who was compelled to it by necessity, as he knew of Northumberland's defeat.

But when Lady Jane received the haughty Mary, and laid her crown at her feet, with the sweet humility, equally free from meanness or fear, Mary seemed struck with the greatness of her manner; her eyes were disarmed, for a moment, of that fierce anger, which flashed from them at her entrance; and filled with a sentiment of admiration, mixed with envy, that vice of little minds, which cannot yield an entire and unpolluted tribute of praise to virtue, she affected to treat her as a poor deluded child, the object only of her contempt, and beneath her anger.

On Mary's entrance into the Tower, she also enquired what prisoners of state were there, and demanded to see them; they presented themselves to her, and she pardoned them all; among the rest the Duke of Norfolk and Courtney.

Mary was exceedingly struck with the person of the latter, and though unacquainted with the manners and ceremonies of the court, the ease and dignity that are natural to him, she thought far preferable to the artful address of the courtier.

She immediately reinstated Norfolk and him into their honors and estates, and created Courtney Earl of Devonshire. — No nobleman about the court is at present in such high favor with the Queen, and all the ladies of it; he has began to apply himself to learn those accomplishments, and active exercises, which his long captivity has withheld from him the means of acquiring.

It is imagined, by some people, that the Queen is strongly attached to him; and, as his rank is noble, and he is an Englishman, it is thought, she will contrive that an alliance with him shall be proposed to the people.

And now, my fair friend, you tremble for your lover; yet comfort yourself, and do not despair; I am certain he will never marry the Queen. He has privately visited us several times; he has informed us of every thing doing at court, and declares that he could not, without the greatest aversion, consider Mary in the light of a wife, was he not engaged to you by every tie of honor and affection.

He speaks highly of the Princess as a friend, who possesses eminent virtues and merit, but says, he shall never cease to love his Laurana, in preference to all the women he ever saw; though he acknowledges, that he fears the Queen will never permit him to marry you. He entreats me to renew to you his vows of eternal constancy. He says, he shall rejoice if the Queen will appoint him any foreign service, which may enable him to see you again, but he fears she will not suffer him to quit the kingdom.

He would request your return to England, but that he should be fearful of your safety, if the Queen, by any means, discovered your connection: this has hitherto prevented his writing to you; but he says, he will now write to you himself, and enclose his letter in mine. You may now, therefore, correspond through this medium; for to own the truth, Mary does really love the Earl, and her temper is suspicious to a great degree.

I am rejoiced to find, by the return of your conductor, that your voyage was agreeable, and that you are settled in a convent at Florence, which you knew something of. — I am impatient for a more particular account of your health, and enjoyment of some share of tranquility.

Adieu,

Anne Grey [Lane, Vol. II 10].

In her reply to Lady Anne, Laurana speaks of the danger of remaining in England, collateral corroboration of her secret affection for Edward Courtenay.

I promised you, my dear Lady Anne, in the short letter which I writ you, by the person sent to conduct me to this convent, a longer one very soon, though I have not yet received one from you.

I will proceed to inform you of a circumstance, which is a very pleasing one to me; it is, that I have found a cousin in the convent I am in. — Heaven surely directed me here for consolation! — My parents lost to me by death, torn by a cruel necessity from that lover, and those dear, and newly acquired friends, I possessed in the queen and yourself, my fate seemed peculiarly cruel during my voyage.

Your excellent Lady Jane had restored to me the patrimony of my parents, so that I obtained a friendly reception from the abbess, from whom I concealed my real name; but for some time, my heart was ready to break, from the consideration of the happiness I had lost, and the lonely, and comfortless situation I was in. — My mind too enlightened, to relish the dull and superstitious routine of a convent life; the cold and formal prayers, so frequently offered by the lips, whilst the heart is absent and unaffected; disgusted by the malevolent passions, and petty competitions, and all the uninteresting events of the nunnery, as well as the mean and artful methods which they took, to induce me to assume the veil.

I most earnestly wished, at times, that I had taken a lodging in England; but perfectly convinced how dangerous, and disagreeable, my unprotected state would have been, utterly ignorant as I am of the world, I was restrained by this consideration from returning.

My mind was in this disgusted situation, when one day, a nun, who had always been inclined to show me every proof of friendship, and whose pleasing person and manner attracted my regard, observing a picture on my bracelet, which was that of my father, suddenly became pale as death, trembled, and was ready to faint: I had remarked her attention to the picture, and much alarmed at the emotion it was the occasion of, flew to assist her, and when a little returned to herself, at my earnest request, she told me that the picture I wore, was that of an uncle extremely dear to her, but whose severity had caused her great and heavy afflictions.

"You are then my cousin," said I, transported with delight, "how happy am I to find so near a relation in a person, for whom I felt a peculiar partiality; I shall now find my situation less painful to me! — How long is it since I have known the sweet pleasure of family connections! Refuse me not your love, my dear cousin, though my father *did* treat you severely; and repose so much confidence in me, as to make me acquainted with my family affairs and connections, to which I am entire stranger."

"Is it possible, my dear, that you are not acquainted with the reason of your father's quitting Florence! — But you shall hear my sad and affecting story — at present, however, you must excuse it; my spirits are overcome with the surprise, pain, and joy which I received at the sight of the picture, and the certainly that the wearer of it is my cousin.

"Yes, my dear Laurana, you do posses my sincerest affection; my heart was also attracted to you from the first moment you entered the convent; greatly was I charmed with your person and manners, and affected at your dejection of spirits. — I often tried to account to myself, for my irresistible prepossession in your favor, but could not do it; but I now discern it to be the effect of natural sympathy, that your happiness interested me, as much as if you had been a sister, though you were so lately a stranger to me.

— May a firm and lasting friendship unite us, and render this abode of melancholy gloom more pleasing to us both."

My cousin, who goes by the name of sister Clara, is about twenty-eight; her person a feminine likeness of my father, but a much greater sweetness diffused over her countenance; her complexion is clear, but pale; and her eyes languidly beautiful; her whole form elegant and interesting, though wrap up in the dress of a nun. She has worn the veil nearly ten years, and is universally beloved by all the deserving part of the convent.

The next day, she came into my room, and told me, that she would relate to me the events of her life, which, with many interruptions from her feelings, she did as follows:

"Your father, my dear Laurana, was the only surviving one of many brothers which mine had, and, at his decease, which I was too young to remember any thing of, he put my fortune and myself into his guardianship, who had not then been long married. I was treated by both your father and mother, with great tenderness; had every proper advantage of education and grew up exceedingly happy under their protection.

When I was about seventeen, I was one evening walking with my governess by the water-side, and was accosted by some fellows in a boat, that was rowing by me, in a very licentious manner, though they wore the dress of gentlemen. I was immediately retiring, when one of them jumped out and was attempting to seize me and place me in the boat; when a gentleman, who had been sitting on a bench, with a book in his hand, suddenly flew to my assistance, and rescued me in a moment from the ruffian, by striking him down with a stick which he held, and, before any of the others had power to go to his assistance, carried me off.

A service so signal, gave the young man a genteel reception with my uncle an aunt, and made no small impression on my young heart, which had never before felt the tender passion.

He was received as a welcome guest whenever he visited us, and soon found means of informing and persuading me of his violent attachment, and obtained the return he wished for; yet it was a long time, however, before he would speak himself to my uncle, or allow me to mention our mutual affection to my aunt.

He said, as his family was of much higher rank than ours, he was certain his father would never consent to the alliance, nor in that case, could I suppose, my friends would permit him to visit me; that, therefore, if I did not think to be separated for ever from him, we must be silent, and conceal our connection.

After some time, I was sought in marriage by a considerable nobleman, whom I refused; at which my uncle was exceedingly enraged, and insisted on my recalling my refusal, and marrying him. He was, indeed, in point of person, fortune, and character, unexceptionable, had I not unhappily been pre-engaged; but this also I refused to do: for though I always considered my uncle as another father, I did not think his authority extended so far, as to control my inclination, in an affair where the happiness of my life was concerned.

Fired to an extreme degree at this opposition to his will, he accused me of carrying on an intrigue with the Count de R-.

I was so much irritated at this accusation, that, I believe, I said some provoking things on the subject. I was conscious of his honor, and my own virtue, and could not support the idea of being suspected of the contrary, and, perhaps, said more than I ought.

My uncle went immediately to the Count's father, and acquainted him with what he suspected of our mutual attachment; not that I think he believed, nor certainly would he have insinuated to him, that our connection was a dishonorable one; but that there was any connection, was enough for the enraged father of the Count; whose pride was extreme, and who had the most ambitious views for his son.

He immediately sent for him into his presence; accused him of this affair, and told him, that unless he would consent to give it instantly up, by the same hour the next evening, he would insist on his taking the habit, and would make his brother his sole heir.

The Count was thunder-struck at this communication, though it was what he had every reason to expect from his father, should he be informed of his attachment.

He remonstrated all in his power, and respectfully entreated his haughty father to see the object of his affection, but all in vain; neither the rank nor fortune was equal; and those were the only things worthy of estimation in his eyes.

He could not see me that evening, and, therefore, wrote to entreat my consent to the only thing that could possibly soften his father in my favor, who, he was persuaded, when he knew it was irretrievable, would become reconciled to the alliance: a private marriage was what he proposed, but he forbore to say what his father had threatened him with.

His eloquence was all-prevailing with me, though I have, a thousand times since, condemned my conduct. I met him early the next morning, and sat off with him to some distance from Florence, where we could be privately married.

By some means, or other, our route was traced, and the enraged father of my lover pursued us, accompanied by my uncle, and the ceremony was just finished, when they entered the church in which we were.

Claps of thunder, and the elements in the utmost fury, could not have appalled us so much as this intrusion. My lover knew his doom. — His father forced him from me; but I became insensible, by violent faintings, and could not be removed for many hours; fits succeeding each other with violence, threatened to tear the agonized soul from its feeble tenement.

At length, I was conducted home, and threatened to be put into a convent, if I did not conceal this contract of marriage, which they both pretended to believe was not concluded when they arrived, and consent the next day to listen to the gentleman whom my uncle had designed for me.

My soul turned with horror from this proposal, and I refused to quit my apartment, where I spent a week in an agony, which language, the most expressive would fail in describing.

At the end of that time I received a letter from my husband, saying, that, after a deal of threatening and persuasion, his father had disinherited him, and turned him from his house; but that he had a small estate, which he could not rob him of, being a legacy left him by a friend. That this little annuity, with me, would be riches to him, if I would condescend to fly with him to Geneva, or some cheap place, where we might live on it, with frugality, in felicity.

That he had empowered his friend, in whose hands it was, to remit to us the income of it quarterly; that for his part, he should regret nothing but my being reduced to poverty, and denied those elegancies which I had been accustomed to.

Transported with joy at this letter, I instantly packed up what clothes I could, and all my jewels, and sent them, in small parcels, by my woman, who had been my confident, and was resolved to share my destiny, by attending me in my flight.

We left the house in the evening; my husband met us, and we traveled incessantly till we thought ourselves out of danger of a second pursuit, before we ventured to take any rest or refreshment.

We arrived safely at Geneva, found out a beautiful little cottage, near the lake, where we settled, and found that sincere happiness, which can only be enjoyed in the married state, where love and friendship intermingle their garlands. The only alloy to it, which I felt, was the consideration that my husband had forfeited his father's blessing and inheritance, which obliged him to worse accommodations than his high birth had accustomed him to.

After some time had expired, however, I observed that my husband became thoughtful and melancholy. He was frequently subject to an absence of thought in conversation, and no longer enjoyed his usual amusements.

My heart, fond of him to destruction, took the alarm, nor would I permit him to rest, till I had obtained the cause of his uneasiness, which arose from his having offended his father, and forfeited his favor and blessing.

He said, he did not regard his being cut off from his inheritance, but he could not support the idea of his father dying, and leaving his with his curse on his head; and he longed to go and throw himself at his feet, and, if possible, get this imprecation recalled, or otherwise could enjoy no peace, though otherwise as blest as man could be.

I did not oppose his journey, and he left me. O fatal hour when I permitted him to do it! but to see him miserable! — him for whom I would have gladly sacrificed my own existence! — it was not in nature. A most mournful farewell did we take of each other.

I wanted to accompany him, but he would not suffer it, and he went attended only by his faithful valet.

An age of time I thought had passed before I heard any intelligence of or from him, and when I did hear from him, it was the happy tidings, that his father was reconciled to him, and approved of his choice; and that the bearer of this letter was to convey me to Florence.

You may imagine that my joy was without bounds. But I must pursue my husband's footsteps for a while, and pass over my own feelings.

His journey was a gloomy one, full of apprehensions, though without shrinking for a moment from his purpose.

He arrived at his father's house, and demanded to see him. — He was introduced to a man whose vindictive rage, and offended pride, were painted in every feature of his face.

He accosted him in the humblest manner on his knees, and implored him to pardon a son, who had never before willfully offended him; who was impelled, by a fatal attachment, to disobey him, but could enjoy no happiness while under a father's interdiction.

Unsoftened by all his prayers and remonstrance's, his features relinquished nothing of their angry expression, but rather became more inflamed.

He told him, he had no other alternative for him now, but to take religious orders; and he would be confined in the house that night, and the next day sent to the convent. That if he complied with this his fixed determination, discovered suitable penitence, perhaps he might one day forgive him.

He was taken forcibly from his father's presence, like a convict, and conducted to his apartment, where, the next day, a monk was sent to him, and endeavored to persuade him to make his peace with his father, and consent to enter into religious orders.

But all his endeavors to that effect being vain, the artful priest took another method to prevail on him:

He went to him a few hours after, with great appearance of joy and friendship in his countenance, and told him, his father would consent to see his wife; and if he approved of her conversation and behavior, he would be reconciled to him and the alliance.

My husband, rejoiced almost to distraction, and totally off his guard, said, he would set out immediately for Geneva and fetch her.

"And is she really so far off as Geneva? said the monk. The count satisfied him with the greatest minuteness where she was, and the monk told him, that he would hasten and inform his father where his wife resided, who would, he doubted not, send for her immediately. The Count was eagerly urging his own departure for that purpose, but the monk was out of the room in an instant.

He immediately went and communicated to the Count's father, the artifice he had used, to obtain the knowledge of my abode. "And now, Seignior," said he, "you may either send for her and confine her, and thus separate them for ever; or, you may threaten him with whatever you please, to obtain of your son, his consent to become a monk.

The father was delighted with this scheme, and thought, at all events, he ought to secure me in his power, and therefore sent for me; ordering his son to write to me, and to advise me to enter into a convent for a little while, till my uncle also could be talked to, and persuaded to be reconciled to me.

Thus, you see my husband himself assisted to throw me into their snares; but, incapable himself of such villainy, he little suspected his father could be guilty of it.

As to myself, my husband's handwriting left me without any doubt on my mind. I settled my little affairs, and sat out with the highest satisfaction; yet, I left my neat little cottage with regret, where I had enjoyed so much real felicity. I was safely conducted to the convent; where I hourly waited, with the utmost impatience, to see again my husband.

The Duke, satisfied that he had me in safety, never thought of seeing me, or concerning himself any more about me, only to order the superior, not to admit any visitors to me, but what came from himself.

The Duke, and his vile agent, then pursued their scheme, acquainting the poor deluded son, that all he had said, was to get his pretended wife into his power; and that now he expected that he would obey him, and determine on a conventual life, for that he never again would see his mistress; and if he did not consent, her situation would be far from agreeable.

Irritated by violent contending passions; filled with all the rage that could animate a human breast, at this injurious treatment; and feeling the utmost contempt for that state of life, which produced such a villain as the monk, he gave vent to all the indignation it inspired him with, in the most furious and unrestrained language; then, snatching up his sword, which he saw at the farther end of the room, on a chair, he plunged it through his body, with that haste and violence, that he fell down before his persecutors had time to fly and prevent him.

The monk hastily quitted the apartment: the haughty Duke, as if struck through the heart with remorse, stood immovably fixed to the place, till my husband, in a faint voice, earnestly requested that he might be permitted to see his wife before he died.

Roused by this request, he bid his servant, who was in the room, to go and conduct me to him, and also to order a surgeon immediately, who soon came, but found it was too late to do any thing for his recovery, the wound being undoubtedly mortal.

Overwhelmed with horror and distress, I received this dreadful intelligence, at the very moment when I expected to see my dear husband enter, full of transport and felicity: but the sight of the man, dear to me as my life, weltering in his blood; struck by his own rash hand, and about to quit me for ever, was a sight too dreadful to support, and the recollection affects me too much to enlarge on it.

He died the next day, penitent, and full of remorse for his precipitation.

The unhappy father bitterly repented of his cruelty. He sent for my uncle, and offered to settle whatever he thought proper on me, and to consider me as his daughter.

But I resolutely refused his offered bounty, and persisted in taking the veil, and ending my days, which I hoped would not be long, in this convent.

My uncle deeply felt this melancholy scene, and regretted, with extreme sorrow and self-condemnation, the part he had it its promotion, by obliging me to quit his house, to avoid a hated alliance.

He entreated me to return to his house with him, and promised, I believe with great sincerity, that he would contribute every thing in his power to restore my spirits, and render me happy.

I told him, there was no happiness for me on earth, and a life of religious retirement was the only state which suited, and would, in any respect, sooth my grief.

I soon after returned to my convent, and, at the end of my novicate, took the veil, in the presence of my relations.

My uncle regretting so much, even to the last, my resolution, that he was disgusted with Florence, and went to reside in England; to which he was still farther induced, by the horrid situation of my husband's father, whose distraction of mind was of the most dreadful nature, uttering vengeance from Heaven on himself and the monk, whom he never after would suffer in his sight.

My husband was his favorite son, and he had always treated him with great affection; but his pride of birth, his son's opposition to his will, and to the schemes he had been for many years planning to aggrandize him, all crushed at once, by his marriage with me, so overcame parental tenderness, and wounded his haughty spirit, that he felt no concern for his happiness, and sought nothing but to hide him in the obscurity of a convent, that he might transfer all his lofty schemes to his brother.

But the fatal end of his unhappy son dissipated his ambitious views, mortified his pride, and awoke his soul to all a father's tenderness; and the remorse consequent to his cruelty to a son so amiable, shook his reason, and destroyed his intellects, for he never again recovered them, but death, a few years after, dissolved his worn-out frame, and his freed soul entered into the presence of his Maker.

It was a long time before I recovered my tranquility, or could raise wishes and views beyond this frail mortality, though I had nothing to attract me to it, nothing to engage my affections. The past, not the future, possessed my thoughts, tied me down to vain regret and discontent; and, alas, how far is this from that disposition which constitutes a real devotee.

I have, however, for some years past, been tolerably composed; but shall I own, My Laurana, that the sight of you, and the picture of my uncle, has brought to my too lively recollection the past events of my life, and renewed my sad regrets. Nor has this relation of them to you tended, in a small degree, to this end.

Ah! would Heaven be pleased to conclude my tiresome warfare, and place me above the reach of restless discontent and useless regrets.

You have the world before you — you are again to put out to sea, and struggle with the billows of life. Ought I not rejoice, that I am in a secure haven, and have only the acquisition of patience and resignation to attain for a little, a very little time, when I shall only have the narrow gulph of death to cross, and then be happy for ever.

My cousin finished her story with tears, which had frequently interrupted her in her narration, and mine slowed plentifully in sympathy with her. You will not, I am certain, refuse her your compassion and esteem.

I must now close this long letter; may I soon receive yours. I am anxious to hear what is become of the Earl of Devonshire, as I have not yet heard from him. Adieu. May all happiness attend my dear Lady Anne and her friends.

Laurana de M-

P.S. I have received your, and the Earl's letters — am shocked and grieved at their contents. The disposition of Lady Jane, the death of the Duke of Northumberland, and the danger of all your friends concerned in her party. — O, what shall I say to console you? Let us hope that Heaven will not permit such virtue as Lady Jane's to suffer; and yet is virtue an exemption from suffering on earth? — Alas, no. How many fatal proofs have I had of that? I cannot deny that I tremble also for my Courtney. Impatiently shall I wait for your letters. Do not fail to write me by every possible conveyance.

Farewell [Lane, Vol. II 19].

Lady Anne's letter to Lady Laurana mentions the need to keep their correspondence a secret from Mary. Had Mary intercepted any of the letters, their fate could have been grim.

I am exceedingly glad, my dear friend, that you have mine and the Earl's letters, both, as the proofs of his constancy have given relief to the anxieties of your mind, in some degree, and because we were very fearful that they had been intercepted by the Queen, whose jealously causes her to set spies on all his actions.

Her hatred to the Lady Elizabeth increases daily, and the friends of that Princess are apprehensive that her life is in danger. She has caused overtures of marriage to be made to Devonshire, who has rejected them in a manner, as little offensive to the Queen's pride and love as possible; yet she is highly enraged with him, though her pride will not suffer her to discover her disappointment publicly; and, I think, the Earl had best quit the kingdom as soon as possible.

He has recovered his health, but a look of dejection hangs over his blooming countenance, which he takes evident pains to conceal. He is become particularly expert in all the manly exercises of youth, and experiences a still greater degree of pleasure in them, from his having been so many years deprived of them. Yet those years of confinement was not lost time to him, but were diligently applied to the cultivation of his mind, of his patience, fortitude, habits of reflection, and philosophy, and convinced him of the vanity of greatness and ambition; though of a faith contrary to my own, I have the charity to believe him beloved by heaven; and as for him, he has too much liberality of mind to be a bigot, and despises sincerely Mary's ignorance and blind zeal.

I think, that to abjure a religion, let it be what it will, in which your conscience still acquiesces, is a meanness that I should scorn myself, or any of my friends for doing; but, if those friends thought me in error, and persuaded me to hear arguments on the other side, I would not shut my ears to conviction, but use every method, by the reason which God hath given me, to discern the truth.

I would not have the Scriptures of *truth* concealed from me in a language I did not understand, but with them in my hand, I would pray for enlightened grace to understand them aright. Thus, it is my opinion, we shall either be preserved from error, or (provided our lives are virtuous) our errors will be harmless.

But not so the Queen; she has refused to hear any arguments in favor of the reformation; she has abolished the laws of Edward, and restored the Romish religion, which last, as a Catholic, you will be pleased at; but when I tell you that she has began a cruel persecution, and that many bishops, and even many of our sex, have sealed their testimony to the belief of the Protestant faith with their blood! Will not your gentle nature revolt at the horrid idea? Will prejudices, imbibed in infancy, so totally warp the nat- ural sensibility of your temper, as to occasion no feelings of detes- tation for a persecuting spirit and pity for the noble sufferers?

Ah! my friend, you have undergone an irksome captivity for your own faith, and from Protestants too. How injurious to any cause, persecution wherever found. How contrary to the genius of true religion. — Can that be truth, which fear exacts from the pro- fessing lip? Can persecution work conviction in the heart? Or frail men imagine they can perform the work of God?

I am very glad you have found a near relation, and amiable friend, in your solitude, my dear Laurana. Her story is, indeed, a melancholy one: — may she find every consolation that is in the power of religion to give her.

Lord Guildford is more reconciled to his father's fate; and all my dear friends begin so far to recover their usual tranquility, as to reassume their usual employments and studies; as the Queen has released them, and permitted them to return to their habitation in town: but the instability of the times, and the gloomy prospects which we have before us, have led us rather to fix on those studies, which will invigorate our minds with fortitude and true philoso- phy, to encounter whatever trials may be appointed us.

From the life and sufferings of the divine founder of our faith, and his faithful martyrs, and the noble lessons imparted to us by them, in that treasury of divine knowledge withheld from you by mercenary priests; by these we have the most effectual instruc- tions in fortitude: greatly do I fear, that we shall need all the aids they can give us. — Alas! Mary, whose resentments are implaca- ble, has not spared my young friends, I fear, but from political rea- sons.

Forgive me, my friend, the melancholy letters I write you: how pleasing and delightful would be the present scene before me, might I hope their happiness would continue.

Beloved and affectionate parents, in the Duke and Duchess of Suffolk. A married pair, inspired with all the tender assiduity and ardor of lovers, in Lord Guildford and Lady Jane: while your friends loses almost the thoughts of her own concerns, in contemplating their felicity and dreading a reverse. They have, however, an allay to their comfort, in the illness of Lady Catherine, who is still at S-, as her weakness will not permit her to travel.

I have not yet quitted them, but my father wishes for some share of my company, and I cannot be so lost to the duty and affection I owe him, as not to attend him.

I am, with sincere regard, dear Lady Laurana,

Your Anne Grey [Lane, Vol. II 63].

Little information has come down about the trial of Lady Jane. No transcript is known to exist, other than the notes indexed in the Additional Manuscript collection (article 10617) in the British Museum.

Not until after the Queen's coronation was Lady Jane brought to trial. On November 13, she and Guildford Dudley, Archbishop Cranmer, and the lords Ambrose and Henry Dudley were taken from the Tower under a guard of four hundred men and arraigned for high treason at the Guild-hall "for having levied war against the Queen, and conspired to set up another in her room." They all pleaded guilty, and the sentence passed upon them was subsequently confirmed by attainder in Parliament (Bayley 427).

Few accounts remain of the trial; Bayley's is the most vivid of them.

Lady Jane appeared before her judges in all her wonted loveliness: her fortitude and composer never forsook her; nor did the throng and bustle of the court, the awful appearance of the seat of judgment, or the passing of the solemn sentence of the law, seem to disturb her mind: of their native bloom her cheeks were never robbed, nor did her voice seem once to falter: on the beauteous traitress every eye was fixed; and the grief that reigned throughout the whole assembly bespoke a general interest in her fate: indeed,

> "Her very judges wrung their hands for pity:
> Their old hearts melted in 'em as she spoke,
> And tears ran down upon their silver beards.
> E'en her enemies were moved, and for a moment
> Felt wrath suspended in their doubtful breasts,
> And questioned if the voice they heard were mortal" [Bayley 428].

Lady Jane and Guildford were found guilty of treason and sentenced to death; but, at the time, they believed Mary might forgive them and release them to lead a private life. That changed soon, as news of the impending marriage of Mary to Spain's King Philip spread through the kingdom. The reports caused disturbances throughout the realm, since many disapproved of a foreigner marrying into their royalty. Small rebel groups formed, opposing the marriage. The most noteworthy leader among them was Sir Thomas Wyatt, sometimes described as a wild man. He sought and eventfully obtained a promise of support from the Duke of Suffolk on the understanding that Lady Jane should be put forward as the claimant to the throne in his proclamation.

The Duke of Suffolk issued his anti-Spanish proclamation in two locations on January 26, 1554, as did Wyatt's heralds at Maidstone. A counter-proclamation was issued at West-Malling after Wyatt departed, and Lady Jane was named the queen's rival, based on Wyatt's intent to restore her. The following day, a government proclamation appeared in several rebellious counties pronouncing Suffolk, Carew, and Wyatt conspirators and traitors to the crown.

Suspicions also arose about a conspiracy between Edward Courtenay and Elizabeth to dethrone Mary and put Elizabeth on the throne, after which Edward would marry her. As Mary's suspicions of her opponents grew, so did the number of prisoners in the Tower and the quantity of blood spilled on the Tower Green, statistics which would continue to rise.

In early January, Lady Anne wrote Lady Laurana, describing the beginning of those conflicts in the first part of the letter. In the second part, written after a short interval, she gave more details

Again is this unhappy kingdom torn to pieces by a civil war. — The Queen is about to form a Spanish alliance: the people are incensed at it, as Don Philip is a foreigner and a Catholic, and have been induced to take up arms: in many different counties are they shedding each other's blood with utmost violence. — How pro-

phetic my fears, that we should not long enjoy the peaceful domestic pleasures which I described to you in my last letter.

The Duke of Suffolk has quitted us for some days past: we have
a thousand apprehensions, lest he should be persuaded to join the
insurgents. The Duchess has sent messengers every where, but
cannot hear any tidings of him, where he usually resorted.

Both Lady Jane, and her Lord, most sincerely wish their father
to forbear all pursuits of ambition, by which his family have suffered so much: he is not formed for them: in domestic life he is
truly amiable; there he shines in every character; but he has never
yet done so in a public one. We all, with the greatest impatience,
wait the return of the messengers.

Since I wrote the above, the Earl of Devonshire has been here,
and has confirmed our fears; informing us, that the Duke has
indeed been prevailed on to join the male-contents. As soon as he
heard of it, he flew to acquaint us with it, and prepare us for what
might be the event. I cannot describe to you the grief of this family,
and our suspense is almost intolerable.

Lord Guildford is very desirous of joining his father-in-law,
but we all, with the greatest earnestness, entreat he will not. My
father and uncle are with him, I find, which distracts me a thousand fears for their safety.

I will not conclude this letter, till I have further information;
God grant it may be fortunate. Adieu.

(continuation)

Ah, my friend! new scenes of horror are preparing for us. My
silence has been a long one, and the vicissitudes numerous, which
have filled up the time since I began this letter. The consequent
alarm, and anxious suspense in which it has kept my mind, would
not permit me to finish it.

The Duke of Norfolk is taken, in endeavoring to raise the people of Warwick and Leicester, where his interest lay. He was pursued at the head of three hundred horse, obliged to disperse his
followers, and fly to conceal himself; but his concealment was
soon discovered, and he was carried prisoner to London.

As the Duke was encouraged to join the rebels by their promises to restore Lady Jane, if they succeeded, to the throne, you may
imagine that the Queen's resentment is highly irritated against
him and his family. The other male-contents are also subdued; and
Sir Thomas Wyatt, the principle instigator of the rebellion, is con-

demned and executed. Four hundred persons are said to have suffered in this insurrection, and as many more were pardoned by the
Queen, to whom they were conducted with ropes about their
necks.

I have no hope remaining, that either the Duke of Suffolk, or
his children, will be spared; and this afflicted, though innocent
family, are now waiting, with painful suspense, the fate of their
husband and father, and their own. — I also dread lest my father
should share the same unhappy fate. I flew to enquire for him, but
found he was not yet taken. — O, that he may escape!

And now, my dear Lady Laurana, prepare your heart; you have
need also of fortitude, if you love the Earl of Devonshire: the vindictive Queen has again sent him into confinement, though perfectly innocent of the crime with which he is charged.

On the examination of Wyatt, he had accused the Lady Elizabeth, and the Earl of Devonshire, as accomplices; but on the scaffold, acquitted them, before the people, of having any share in his
rebellion. However, on his first accusation of them, Mary immediately had her sister arrested, under a strong guard, and sent to the
Tower; here, however, she did not stay long; the dying declaration
of Wyatt, obliged the Queen to release her: but she soon after
found a pretence to imprison her again, and sent her to Woodstock; and also confined the Earl, though equally innocent, in
Fotheringay Castle. — What havoc does human passion cause in
the world, unguided by wisdom and virtue!

I will write to you again, if I am able to do so, when the cup of
fate is filled. — I cannot afford you any consolation at present, my
friend; horrible images of death present themselves continually
before my eyes.

How earnestly do I pray for the fortitude of Lady Jane. — How
do I admire her noble steady mind, rising with a divine radiance,
above the thick cloud of fate which hovers around her. — When
will it break! When will the thunder burst from it, which thus
oppresses us with its intolerable weight! — O God! prepare us for
the event!

Anne Grey [Lane, Vol. II 74].

At about that time, though the exact date is not known, Lady
Jane and Guildford wrote notes in the lower margins of a prayer
book, "A vellum Book of a small but thick size, being the Manual of
Devotions of some English Protestant of Quality, who was cast into

Prison wrongfully, according to his own Opinion. It was illuminated by some foreigner, but hath since been abused, & is now imperfect in two places" (Harley, Vol. II 659).

After a notation, items 36, 37 and 38 describe the notes penned by Jane and Guildford in the lower margins of the book. The book is currently on display in the British Library.

> I will not affirm that this Manual was written by the Direction of Edward Seymour Duke of Somerset & Protector of England, upon his first Commitment to the Tower of London, and that the last five Prayers were added after his second Commitment, which ended in his Execution. But if this were so, 'tis easy to apprehend how it might come into the hands of that noble but unfortunate Lady, the Lady Jane Grey: whose Marriage with the Lord Guildford Dudley, fourth son to the ambitious Duke of Northumberland cost them all their Lives. But that this Book was in the Lady Jane's hands or possession, and was also looked into by her Husband, appears by the 3 following Notes, written in the lower Margins.
>
> 36. "Your loving and obedient son which unto your Grace long life in this world, with as much joy & comfort, as ever I wish to my self; and in the world to come joy everlasting. Your most humble son until his Death G. Dudley."   59.b.
>
> 37. "Forasmuch as you have desired so simple a woman to write in so worthy a book, good Master Lieutenant, therefore, I shall, as a friend desire you, and as a Christian require you, to call upon God, to incline your heart to his laws, to quicken you in his way, and not to take the word of truth utterly out of your mouth. Live still to die, that by death you may purchase eternal life; and remember how the end of Mathew, who as we read in the scriptures, was the longest liver that was of a man, died at the last. For, as the Preacher sayeth, there is a time to be born, and a time to die; and the day of Death is better than the day of our birth. Yours as the Lord knoweth as a friend. Jane Dudley."   74.b.
>
> The Gentleman this was written for, seems to have been Sir John Gage Lieutenant of the Tower of London, when she was prisoner therein.
>
> 38. "The lord comfort your Grace, and that in his word wherein all creatures only are to be comforted. And though it hath pleased God to take away 2 of your children: yet think not, I most humbly beseech your Grace, that you have lost them; but trust that we by leasing this mortal life, have won an immortal Life. And I, for my

part, as I have honored your Grace in this life, will pray for you in another Life. Your Graces humble daughter Jane Dudley."

None of these 3 Notes or Epistles are mentioned by any of our Historians, that I now remember [Harleian, Vol II 659].

The following letter appears to come from about the same time. From John Banks to Henry Bullinger, dated at London, March 15, 1554, it appears in *Original Letters relative to the English Reformation*, by the Rev. Hastings Robinson, D.D. F.A.S., letter CXLI, page 303. Banks writes,

"Moreover, it may be seen how her [Lady Jane] truly admirable mind was illuminated by the light of God's word, by two letters, one of which she herself wrote to the Lady Catherine, her sister, a most noble virgin, to inspire her with a love of the sacred writings, and the other to a certain apostate, to bring him back to Christ the Lord."

Doctor Harding (1516–1572), later the antagonist of Bishop Jewel, received the following letter from Lady Jane.

So oft as I call to mind (dear friend and chosen brother) the dreadful and fearful sayings of God, that he which layeth hold upon the plough and looketh back again, is not meet for the kingdom of heaven; and on the other side to remember the comfortable words of our Savior Christ, to all those that forsaking themselves do follow him, I cannot but marvel at thee and lament thy case; that thou, which sometimes wert the lively member of Christ, but now the deformed imp of the devil; sometimes the beautiful temple of God, but now the stinking and filthy kennel of Satan; sometimes the unspotted spouse of thy Savior, but now the unshamefast paramour of Antichrist; sometimes my faithful brother, but now a stranger and apostate; yea sometimes my stout Christian solder, but now a cowardly runaway. So oft as I consider the threatenings and promises of the Divine Justice to all those which faithfully love him, I cannot but speak to thee, yea, rather cry out and exclaim against thee, thou seed of Satan, and not of Juda, whom the devil hath deceived, the world hath beguiled, and desire of life hath subverted, and made of a Christian an infidel.

Wherefore hast thou taken upon thee the Testament of the Lord in thy mouth? Wherefore hast thou hitherto yielded thy body to the fire, and to the bloody hands of cruel tyrants? Wherefore hast thou instructed others to be strong in Christ, when thou thyself dost now so horribly abuse the testament and law of the Lord; when thou thyself, preachest (as it were not to steal) yet most abominably stealest, not from men but from God, and as a most heinous sacrilegious robber, robbest Christ thy redeemer of his right in his members, thy body and thy soul; when thou thyself dost rather choose to live miserably (with shame) in this world, than to die gloriously and reign in honor with Christ, to the end of all eternity, in whom even in death there is life beyond wish, beyond all expression; and when, I say, thou thyself art most weak, thou ought to show thy self most strong, for the strength of a fort is known before the assault, but thou yieldest (like a faint captain) thy hold before any battery be brought against thee.

Oh wretched and unhappy man what art thou but dust and ashes, and wilt thou resist thy maker, that formed and fashioned thee: wilt thou now forsake him that called thee from custom gathering among the Romish Antichristians, to be an ambassador and messenger of his eternal word; he that first framed thee, and since thy creation and birth preserved thee, nourished thee, and kept thee, yea, and inspired thee with the spirit of knowledge (I cannot, I would I could say of grace) shall he not possess thee, darest thou deliver up thy self to another, being not thine own but his? How canst thou, having knowledge, or how darest thou neglect the law of the Lord, and follow the vain traditions of men? and whereas thou hast been a public professor of his name, become now a defacer of his glory. I will not refuse the true God, and worship the invention of man, the golden calf, the whore of Babylon, the Romish religion, the abominable idol, the most wicked mass: wilt thou torment again, rent and tear the most precious body of our Savior Christ with thy bodily and fleshy teeth without the breaking whereof upon the cross, our sins and transgressions, could else no way be redeemed? Wilt thou take upon thee to offer up any sacrifice unto God for our sins, considering that Christ offered up himself (as St. Paul saith) upon the Cross, a lively sacrifice once for all.

Can neither the punishment of the Israelites (which for their idolatry so oft they received) move thee; neither the terrible threatenings of the ancient prophets stir thee, nor the crosses of God's own mouth fear thee to honor any other God than him?

Wilt thou so regard him that spared not his dear and only son for thee, so diminishing, yea, utterly extinguishing his glory, that thou wilt attribute the praise and honor to idols, which have mouths and speak not, eyes and see not, ears yet hear not, which shall perish with them that made them: what saith the prophet Baruck, where he reciteth the epistle of Jeremy, written to the captive Jews? Did he not forewarn them that in Babylon they should see gods of gold, silver, wood, and stone, born upon men's shoulders to cause a fear upon the heathen? But be not you afraid of them (saith Jeremy) nor do as others do: but when you see others worship them, say you in your hearts, it is thou (O lord) that oughtest only to be worshipped: for as touching the timber of those gods the carpenter framed them and polished them, yea guilded they be and laid over with silver and vain things and cannot speak: he sheweth moreover, the abuse of their deckings how the priests took off their ornaments, and appareled there woman therewithal: how one holdeth a scepter, another a sword in his hand, and yet can they judge in no matter, nor defend themselves, much less any other, from either hatred or murder, nor yet from gnawing worms, dust, filth, of any other evil thing; these and such like words speaketh Jeremy unto them, whereby he proveth them but vain things, and no gods, and at last he concludeth thus; confounded be those that worship them.

They were warned by Jeremy, and thou as Jeremy hast warned others, and art warned thyself by many Scriptures in many places.

God, saith he, is a jealous God, which will have all honor, glory, and worship given to him only. And Christ saith in the fourth of Luke, to Satan which tempted him, even to the same Satan, the same Beelzebub, the same devil which hath prevailed against thee: it is written (saith he) thou shalt honor the Lord thy God, and him only shalt thou serve.

These and such like do prohibit thee, and all Christians to worship any other God than he which was before all words, and laid the foundations both of heaven and earth, and wilt thou honor a detestable idol invented by the Popes of Rome, and the uncharitable college of politic Cardinals?

Christ offered up himself once for all, and wilt thou offer him up again daily at thy pleasure? but thou wilt say thou doest it for a good intent: Oh sink of sin! Oh child of perdition! canst thou dream of any good intent therein, when thy conscience beareth thee witness of the wrath of God promised against thee?

How did Saul, who for that he disobeyed the word of God for a good intent, was thrown from his worldly and temporal kingdom: shalt thou then which dost so deface God's honor and rob him of his right, inherit the eternal heavenly kingdom? wilt thou for a good intent pluck Christ out of heaven, and make his death void, and deface the triumph of his cross, offering him up daily? wilt thou either for fear of death, or hope of life, deny and refuse thy God, who enriched thy poverty? healed thy infirmity, and yielded to this victory if thou wouldst have kept it? Dost thou not consider that the thread of life hangeth upon him that made thee, who can (as his will is) either twine it hard to last the longer, or untwine it again to break the sooner? Dost thou not remember the saying of David, a notable king, which teacheth thee, a miserable wretch, in his civ Psalm, where he saith, When thou takest away thy spirit, O lord, from men, they die, and are turned again to their dust, but when thou lettest thy breath go forth, they shall be made, and thou shalt renew the face of the earth.

Remember the saying of Christ in his Gospel, whosoever seeketh to save his life shall lose it, but whosoever will lose it for my sake shall find it; and in another place, whosoever loveth father or mother above me, is not meet for me, for he that will be my disciple, must forsake father and mother, and himself, and take up his cross, and follow me: what cross? The cross of infamy and shame, of misery and poverty, of affliction and persecution, for his name sake.

Let the oft falling of those heavenly showers pierce thy stony heart; let the two-edged sword of God's holy word hew asunder the knit-together sinews of worldly respects, even to the very marrow and life blood of thy carnal heart, that thou mayst once again forsake thyself to embrace Christ, and like as good subjects will not refuse to hazard all in the defense of their earthly and temporal governors, so fly not like a white livered milk-sop from the standard, whereby thy chief Captain, Christ, hath placed thee in a noble array of this life; viriliter ago confortetur cor tuum et sustine dominum, fight manfully, come life, come death, the quarrel is God's, and undoubtedly the victory is ours.

But thou wilt say, I will not break unity; what? Not the unity of Satan and his members, not the unity of darkness, the agreement of antichrist and his adherents? Nay, they thou deceives thyself with fond imaginations of such an unity as is amongst the enemies of Christ: were not the false prophets in any unity? Were not Joseph's brethren, Jacob's sons, in an unity? Were not the heathen as the Amelechites, the Peresites and Jebusites in an unity? I keep no order but look rather to my matter: were not the Scribes and Pharisees in an unity? Doth not King David testify, conveniunt in unum adversus Dominum, yea, thieves and murderers, conspirators and traitors have their unity?

Mark my dear friend (yea friend if thou beest not God's enemy,) there is no unity but when Christ knitteth the knot amongst such as be his, yea, be you well assured that where his truth is resident, there it is verified, that he saith, Non veni mittere pacem in terram sed gladium, that is, Christ came to set one against another; the son against the father, the daughter against mother: deceive not thyself therefore with the glistening and glorious name of unity, for antichrist hath his unity, yet not in deed, but in name, for the agreement of evil men is not an unity, but a conspiracy.

Thou hast heard some threatenings, some curses, and some admonishments of the Scriptures, to those who love themselves above Christ.

Thou hast heard also the sharp and biting words to those which deny him for love of life, saith he not, that he which denieth me before men, I will deny him before my father which is in heaven: and to the same effect writeth St. Paul in the vi. to the Hebrews, saying, it is impossible that they which have been once lightened, and have tasted of the heavenly gift of grace, and been made partakers of the Holy Ghost, and have relished of the pure word of God, if they fall and slide away, it is impossible that they should be renewed again by repentance, crucifying again to themselves the Son of God, and making him as it were a mockingstock, or gaud of their fancies. And again, (saith he) if we shall willingly sin after we have received the knowledge of the truth, there is no oblation left for sin, but the terrible expectation of judgment and fire which shall devour the adversaries. Thus St. Paul writeth, and thus thou readest, and dost thou not quake and tremble? Well, if these terrible and thundering alarums cannot stir thee to arise and cleave unto Christ, and forsake the world, yet let the sweet consolations and promises of the Scriptures: let the examples of Christ and his Apostles, both Martyrs and Confessors, encourage thee to take faster hold by Christ. Hearken what he saith again in his holy Gospel; blessed are you when men revile you, and persecute you for my sake, rejoice and be glad, for great is your reward in heaven, for so persecuted they the Prophets before you.

Hear what Esau saith: fear not the curse of men. Be not afraid of their blasphemies and railings, for worms and moths shall eat them up like cloth and wool, but my righteousness shall endure for ever, and my saving health for generation to generation: what are thou then (saith he) that fearest a mortal man, the child of a man, which fadeth away as doth the flower, and forgettest the Lord that made thee, that spread out the heavens like a curtain, and laid the foundations of the earth so sure, that they cannot be removed: I am the Lord thy God, which maketh the sea to rage, and to be still, who is the Lord of hosts; I shall put my word in thy mouth, and defend thee with the turning of a hand. And our Saviour Christ saith to his disciples, they shall accuse you, and bring you before the princes and rulers for my name sake, and some of you they shall persecute and kill: but fear you not (saith he) neither care you not what you shall say, for it is my spirit that speaketh in you, the hand of the highest shall defend you, for the hairs of yours heads are numbered, and none of them shall perish. I have laid up treasure for you (saith he) where no thief can steal, nor moth corrupt, and happy are you if you endure to the end. Fear not them (saith Christ) which have power over the body only, but fear him that hath power both over the body and the soul; the world loveth her own, and if you were of the world the world would love you, but you are mine, and therefore the world doth hate you.

Let these, and such like consolations out of the Scriptures strengthen you o God-ward; let not the examples of holy men and women go out of your mind, as that of Daniel, and the rest of the prophets; of the three children of Eleazarus, that constant father; the Machabees children, that of Peter, Paul, Stephen, and other Apostles and holy Martyrs, in the beginning and infancy of the Church; as of good Simeon, Archbishop of Seloma, and Zetrophone, with infinite others, under Sapores the king of the Persians and Indians, who condemned all torments devised by the tyrants for their Savior's sake.

Return, return again for honor and mercy's sake into the way of Christ Jesus, and as becometh a faithful soldier, put on that armor which St. Paul teacheth to be most necessary for a Christian man, and above all things take to you the shield of faith.

And be you most devoutly provoked by Christ's own example, to withstand the devil, to forsake the world, and to become a true and faithful member of his mystical body, who spared not his own flesh for our sins. Throw down thyself with the fear of his threatened vengeance for this so great and heinous offence of apostasy, and comfort yourself on the other part with the mercy, blood, and promises of him that is ready to turn to you whensoever you turn to him: disdain not to come again with the lost son, seeing you have so wandered with him: be not ashamed to turn again with him from the swill of strangers, to the delicates of the most benign and loving father, acknowledging that you have sinned against heaven and earth; against heaven by staining his glorious name, and causing his most sincere and pure word to be evil spoken of through you, against earth by offending your so many weak brethren to whom you have been a stumbling block through your sudden sliding.

Be not ashamed to come again with Mary, and to weep bitterly with Peter, not only with shedding of tears out of your bodily eyes, but also pouring out the streams of your heart, to wash away, out of the sight of God, the filth and mire of your offensive fall; be not ashamed to say with the publican, Lord be merciful unto me a sinner: remember the horrible history of Julian of old, and the lamentable case of Francis Spira of late, whose remembrance me thinketh should be yet so green to your memory, that being a thing of our time, you should fear the like inconvenience, seeing that you are fallen into the like offence. Last of all, let the lively remembrance of the last day be always before your eyes, remembering the terror that such shall be in at that time, with the runagrates and fugitives from Christ, which setting more by the world than by heaven, more by their life, than by him that gave them their life, more by the vanity of a painful breath, than the perfect assurance of eternal salvation, did shrink: yea, did clean fall away from him that never forsook them. And contrariwise, the inestimable joys prepared for them which feared no peril, nor dreading death, have manfully fought, and victoriously triumphed over all power of darkness; over hell, death, and damnation, through their most redoubted captain Jesus Christ our Saviour, who even now stretcheth out his arms to receive you, ready to fall upon your neck, and kiss you: and last of all, to feast you with the dainties and delicates of his own most precious blood, which undoubtedly, if it might stand with his determinate purpose, he would not let to shed again, rather than you should be lost; to whom with the Father and the Holy Ghost, be all honor, praise, and glory everlasting. Amen.

Yours, if you be Christ's,
Jane Grey.

Postscript.
Be constant, be constant, fear not for pain,
Christ hath deliver'd thee, and heav'n is thy gain.
J.G. [Nicolas 22].

By February 6, the rebellion was crushed, with all the conspirators imprisoned in the Tower, including the Duke of Suffolk. The Duke of Suffolk's involvement sealed Lady Jane's and her husband's fate. One contemporary wrote, "Jane of Suffolk and her husband are to lose their heads" (Chapman LJG, 190).

About that time, Lady Anne wrote to Lady Laurana, describing her despair as the tragic event drew closer. Lady Anne described receiving letters from Jane, at the final hour. Perhaps those are the letters surviving today and also those included in the "Lane Letters."

O my Laurana! the hour of fate approaches: the Queen has sent to demand her prisoners, under a strong guard.

When the Constable of the Tower was introduced to Lady Jane, and declared his commission, she received it with a smiling and placid countenance, professed her readiness to obey the Queen, and be conveyed wherever her majesty thought proper; she only asked an hour to prepare herself, which was complied with.

When we were alone in her apartment, she committed to my charge all her private letters, and copies of her own to me; and other papers, which she had not time to destroy, and did not choose to have seized and exposed. I then entreated her to permit me to attend and remain with her in the Tower, but not all my persuasions could prevail on her to suffer it; "Stay and console my dear mother" she said, "you will both be allowed to visit me again; till then, my dear Lady Anne, adieu. Pray for your unfortunate Jane."

I saw them depart, with the most heart-felt agony of grief, mixed with admiration; but my thoughts were called away from my own sorrows to those of the Duchess, who was distracted with her grief for many hours; I thought she would never recover her senses. — Alas! how little consolation can I afford her, who am myself inconsolable!

Sleep having, however, composed the mind of this unfortunate mother; we went the next day to visit our excellent young friends, and their misguided father; who was filled with the most severe remorse for his late conduct, which had involved those most dear to him in his punishment.

To describe the affecting interview is impossible; nor that noble fortitude displayed in the charming Lady Jane; which does not consist in a stoical apathy of mind, but, though possessed of all the feminine delicacy and sensibility of her sex, towards her parents, husband, and friends, a steady faith, and hope in Heaven, supports her soul, and enables her to view imprisonment, and even the prospect of death, in her own person, without terror; and to posses composure enough to console, exhort, and animate her friends to follow her example, and confirm themselves in her principle.

The Duchess and myself were not permitted to continue in the Tower, but have liberty to visit them every day; which we owe to the compassion of the Constable of the Tower, who seems quite struck and awed by her appearance and behavior.

O, my friend! you know this best of women. You have seen her when elevated to the highest rank; and then admired her humility and affability: how would you now admire her noble and unaffected piety! her indifference to life! her tenderness to her friends! and that sweet consolation, which she affords to her poor father, bent down beneath his grief and regrets!

Lord Guildford seems to have quite forgot all thought or solicitude about himself, and his own approaching fate; all his anxieties, all his attentions, all his grief, is on the account of his almost adored wife: he seems sometimes almost distracted with the idea of her misfortunes, and probably, untimely end.

Ah! how cruel must the Queen discover herself, if she can ever sign the mandate for their death! — But cruel and inhuman she *has* discovered herself, and I cannot deceive myself with the hope, that she will forgive them: the thought sickens my soul with horror. — Alas! perhaps before I write you again, they may be no more!

Anne Grey [Lane, Vol. II 84].

Lady Jane wrote a short letter to her father from the Tower in the last week of January or the first week of February.

Father, although it hath pleased God to hasten my death by you, by whom my life should rather have been lengthened, yet I can so patiently take it, that I yield God more hearty thanks for shortening my woeful days, than if all the world had given into my possession, with life lengthened at my own will. And albeit I am very well assured of your impatient dolor's, redoubled many ways, both in bewailing your own woe, and especially, as I am informed, my woeful estate: yet my dear father, if I may, without offence, rejoice in my own mishaps, herein I may account myself blessed, that washing my hands with the innocence of my fact, my guiltless blood may cry before the Lord, Mercy to the innocent! And yet though I must needs acknowledge, that being constrained, and as you know well enough continually assayed, yet in taking upon me, I seemed to consent, and therein grievously offended the queen and her laws, yet do I assuredly trust that this my offence towards God is so much the less, in that being in so royal estate as I was, my enforced honor never mingled with mine innocent heart. And thus, good father, I have opened unto you the state wherein I presently stand, my death at hand, although to you perhaps it may seem woeful, yet to me there is nothing that can be more welcome than from this vale of misery to aspire to that heavenly throne of all joy and pleasure, with Christ my Savior: in whose steadfast faith, (if it may be lawful for the daughter so to write to the father) the Lord that hath hitherto strengthened you, so continue to keep you, that at the last we may meet in heaven with the Father, Son, and Holy Ghost.

I am,

Your obedient daughter till death,

Jane Dudley [Nicolas 47].

On February 8, Master de Feckenham, Abbot of Westminster, was sent to tell the Lady Jane that she must prepare for death, and Lady Jane transcribed their well-known interview. Mary hoped to convert Jane to the Catholic faith before her execution, but Jane would not convert.

Feckenham. What thing is required in a Christian?

Jane. To believe in God the Father, in God the Son, in God the Holy Ghost, three persons and one God.

Feckenham. Is there nothing else required in a Christian but to believe in God?

Jane. Yes: We must believe in him, we must love him, with all our heart, with all our soul, and all our mind, and our Neighbor as our self.

124

Feckenham. Why then Faith justifieth not, nor saveth not?

Jane. Yes verily, Faith (as Saint Paul saith) only justifieth.

Feckenham. Why Saint Paul saith, if I have all Faith of the World, without love, it is nothing.

Jane. True it is, for how can I love him I trust not, or how can I trust in him whom I love not. Faith and Love ever agree together, and yet Love is comprehended in Faith.

Feckenham. How shall we love our Neighbor?

Jane. To love our Neighbor, is to feed the hungry, clothe the naked, and to give drink to the thirsty, and to do to him as we would do to ourselves.

Feckenham. Why then it is necessary to salvation to do good works, and it is not sufficient to believe?

Jane. I deny that[;] I affirm that faith only saveth: But it is meat for all Christians, in token that they follow their Master Christ, to do good works: yet may we not say, nor in any wise believe, that they profit to salvation: for although we have all done all that we can, yet we are unprofitable servants, and the faith we have only in Christ's blood, and his merits saveth.

Feckenham. How many Sacraments are there?

Jane. Two: the one the Sacrament of Baptism; and the other the Sacrament of the Lord's Supper.

Feckenham. No, there be seven Sacraments.

Jane. By what Scripture find you that.

Feckenham. Well we will talk of that hereafter: But what is signified by your two Sacraments?

Jane. By the Sacrament of Baptism I am washed with Water, and regenerated in the Spirit, and that washing is a token to me that I am the Child of God: The Sacrament of the Lords Supper is offered unto me as a sure Seal and Testimony, that I am, by the blood of Christ which he shed for me on the Cross, made partaker of the everlasting Kingdom.

Feckenham. Why what do you receive in that bread, do you not receive the very body and blood of Christ?

Jane. No surely, I do not believe so, I think at that Supper I receive neither flesh nor blood, but only Bread and Wine, the which bread when it is broken, and the wine when it is drank, putteth me in mind how that for my sins the body of Christ was broken and his blood shed on the cross, and with that bread and wine I receive the benefits which came by breaking

125

of his body, and by the shedding of his blood on the Cross for my sins.

Feckenham. Why but, (Madam) doth not Christ speak these words; Take, eat, this is my body: can you require any plainer words: doth he not say, that it is his body?

Jane. I grant he saith so; and so he saith like wise in other places, I am the Vine, I am the Door, it being only but a figurative borrowed speech: Doth not Saint Paul say that he calleth these things which are not as though they were: God forbid that I should say that I eat the very natural body and blood of Christ: for then either I should pluck away my Redemption, or confess their were two bodies, or two Christ's: two bodies, the one body was tormented on the Cross, and then if they did eat another body, how absurd: again if his body was eaten really, then it was not broken upon the Cross, or if it were broken upon the Cross (as it is doubtless) then it was not eaten of his Disciples.

Feckenham. Why is it not as possible that Christ by his power could make his body both to be eaten and broken, as to be born of a woman without the seed of man, and as to walk on the Sea having a body, and other such like miracles which he wrought by his power only.

Jane. Yes verily, if God would have done at his last supper a miracle, he might have done so: But I say he minded nor intended no work or miracle; but only to break his body and shed his blood on the Cross for our sins: But I beseech you answer me to this one question; Where was Christ when he said: Take, eat, this is my body: was he not at the Table when he said so he was at that time alive, and suffered not till the next day? Well what took he but bread? And what broke he but bread? And what gave he but bread? Look what he took he bake, and look what he bake he gave, and look what he gave did they eat, and yet all this while he himself was at Supper before his Disciples, or else they were deceived.

Feckenham. You ground your Faith upon such Authors as say and unsay, both with a breath, and not upon the Church, to whom you ought to give credit.

Jane. No, I ground my faith upon Gods word, and not upon the Church: for if the Church be a good Church, the faith of the Church must be tried by Gods word, and not Gods words by the church, neither yet my faith: Shall I believe the church

126

because of antiquity; or shall I give credit to that church which taketh away from me a full half part of the Lord's Supper, and will let no layman receive it in both kinds, but the Priests only themselves, which thing if they deny to us, they deny us part of our salvation: And I say that it is an evil and no good Church, and not the spouse of Christ, but the spouse of the Devil, which altereth the Lords Supper, and both taketh from it, and addeth to it: To that Church I say God will add plagues, and from that church will he take their part out of the Book of Life: You may learn of Saint Paul, how he did administer it to the Corinthians in both kinds, which since your Church refuseth, shall I believe it, God forbid?

Feckenham. That was done by the wisdom of the Church, and to a merit good intent to avoid an heresy, which then sprung in it.

Jane. O but the Church must not alter Gods will and ordinances for the color or gloss of a good intent, it was the error of King Saul, and he not only reaped a curse, but perished thereby, as it is evident in the Holy Scriptures.

To this M. Feckenham gave me a long, tedious, yet eloquent reply, using many strong and Logical persuasions, to compel me to have leaned to their Church, but my Faith had armed my Resolution to withstand any assault that words could then use against me: Of many other Articles of Religion we reasoned, but these formerly rehearsed were the chiefest and most effectual.

Subscribed Jane Dudley [Nicolas, Part II, 35].

Lady Jane also composed the following prayer.

O Lord, thou God and father of my life! Hear me, poor and desolate woman, which flyeth unto thee only, in all troubles and miseries. Thou, O lord, art the only defender and deliverer of those that put their trust in thee; and, therefore, I, being defiled with sin, encumbered with affliction, unquieted with troubles, wrapped in cares, overwhelmed with miseries, vexed with temptations, and grievously tormented with the long imprisonment of this vile mass of clay, my sinful body, do come unto thee, O merciful Savior, craving thy mercy and help, without the which so little hope of deliverance is left, that I may utterly despair of my liberty. Albeit, it is expedient, that seeing our life standeth upon trying, we should be visited some time with some adversity, whereby we might both be tried whether we be of thy flock or no, and also know thee and ourselves the better; yet thou that saidst thou wouldst not suffer us to be tempted above our power, be merciful unto me, now a miserable wretch, I beseech thee; which, with Solomon, do cry unto thee, humbly desiring thee, that I may neither be too much puffed up with prosperity, neither too much depressed with adversity; lest I, being too full, should deny thee, my God; or being too low brought, should despair and blaspheme thee, my Lord and Savior. O merciful God, consider my misery, best known unto thee; and be thou now unto me a strong tower of defense, I humbly require thee. Suffer me not to be tempted above my power, but either be thou a deliverer unto me out of this great misery, or else give me grace patiently to bear thy heavy hand and sharp correction. It was thy right hand that delivered the people of Israel out of the hands of the Pharaoh, which for the space of four hundred years did oppress them, and keep them in bondage; let it therefore likewise seem good to thy fatherly goodness, to deliver me, sorrowful wretch, for whom thy son Christ shed his precious blood on the cross, out of this miserable captivity and bondage, wherein I am now. How long wilt thou be absent? — for ever? Oh, Lord! hast thou forgotten to be gracious, and hast thou shut up thy loving kindness in displeasure? wilt thou be no more entreated? Is thy mercy clear gone for ever, and thy promise come utterly to an end for everyone? Why dost thou make so long tarrying? shall I despair of thy mercy? Oh God! Far be that from me; I am thy workmanship, created in Christ Jesus; give me grace therefore to tarry thy leisure, and patiently to bear thy works, assuredly knowing, that as thou canst, so thou wilt deliver me, when it shall please thee, nothing doubting or mistrusting thy goodness towards me; for thou knowest better what is good for me than I do; therefore do with me in all things what thou wilt, and plague me what way thou wilt. Only in the mean time, arm me, I beseech thee, with thy armor, that I may stand fast, my loins being girded about with verity, having on the breast-plate of righteousness, and shod with the shoes prepared by the gospel of peace; above all things, taking to me the shield of faith, wherewith I may be able to quench all the fiery darts of the wicked; and taking the helmet of salvation, and the sword of thy spirit, which is thy most holy word; praying always, with all manner of prayer and supplication, that I may refer myself wholly to thy will, abiding thy pleasure, and comforting myself in those troubles that it shall please thee to send me;

seeing such troubles be profitable for me, and seeing I am assuredly persuaded that it cannot but be well all thou doest. Hear me,
O merciful Father, for his sake, whom thou wouldest should be a
sacrifice for my sins; to whom with thee and the Holy Ghost, be all
honor and glory.

Amen! [Nicolas, part II 49].

Lady Anne attempted to convey her sorrow and despair about
the events that would soon take Lady Jane and her husband's lives,
in the following letter to Lady Laurana, written the day before the
execution. She mentions a letter Lady Jane wrote to her sister
Catherine, the night before the execution; this is followed by a
second from Jane to Catherine.

I am just returned from the Tower, and find my friends have
received a message from the Queen, intimating, that if they will
renounce the Protestant religion, and embrace the Romish faith,
she will grant them a full pardon. This without the least hesita-
tion, they absolutely refused to comply with.

They said, that they were ready to suffer death whenever it
was the Queen's pleasure to inflict it; as it was only an entrance
into a happier life, and would put them into possession of the martyr's crown; but they would never receive their pardon on a condition so unworthy and base, as that of giving up the purity of their
principles to obtain it.

The Queen again sent priests, to endeavor to convert them,
being unwilling, she said, that two young people so amiable
should be lost to salvation by their obstinacy; but I think it is more
probable, that she wanted to render herself popular, by an appar-
ent lenity; but her pious labors were all in vain: no temporal hope,
or fears, can shake the steady souls of Lord Guildford and Lady
Jane. Nor can I wish them to comply, heart-rending as it is, to lose
and survive them: I may, indeed, share the same fate: we know not
how far a furious zeal will carry the bigoted Mary.

God grant I may not render myself unworthy of such noble
friends, by a mean renunciation of the true religion. — how many
bright examples are at present, almost daily displayed, of patient
constancy, in suffering for the truth.

Mary's cruelties have scarcely a parallel; and the pleasure with
which she even gluts her own eyes, with the fight of those noble
martyrs sufferings, betrays the natural barbarity of her disposi-

tion. — Surely; for the scourge of this kingdom, was such a mind placed in a female form; and that female destined by Providence to be Queen of England.

Mary has granted but three days reprieve to my dear young friends; who have defended their religious tenets by all the usual arguments; but they were all thrown away, on blind and unfeeling zealots, and mercenary priests.

Lady Jane has had the equanimity of mind to sit down and write to Lady Catherine, who is still ill, a letter in Greek, in which she exhorted her to maintain, in every fortune, the like steady perseverance; sending her with it, a copy of the Scriptures in that tongue.

I was commissioned to convey to her this letter; but I cannot express how sensible and deeply it affected me, while writing to her, to reflect that she will see her no more! that, in three days, we shall lose for ever, in this world, that amiable pair, by a violent and untimely death! that those beautiful persons, so beloved and admired by all who know them, and destined to be destroyed! Blasted in their full bloom!

How awful are the dispensations of Providence! — How shall I support the dreaded hour of separation! How submit, as I ought, to lose the friend of my youth! dear to me as another self; beloved and cherished beyond any thing on earth! — Cruel doom! Fatal ambition! — how dearly purchased are thy honors? — I can write no more! [Lane, Vol. II 91].

Lady Jane wrote this to her sister, Lady Catherine, the night before her execution, in the end of the New Testament in Greek that Jane had in her possession. Of all the literary remains of Lady Jane, this letter has been reprinted most often.

I have here sent you, my dear sister Catherine, a book, which although it be not outwardly trimmed with gold, or the curious embroidery of the artfulness [of] needles, yet inwardly it is more worth than all the precious mines which the vast world can boast of: it is the book, my only best, and best loved sister, of the law of the Lord: it is the Testament and last will, which he bequeathed unto us wretches and wretched sinners, which shall lend you to the path of eternal joy: and if you with a good mind read it, and with an earnest desire follow it, no doubt it shall bring you to an immortal and everlasting life: it will teach you to live, and learn you to die: it shall win you more, and endow you with greater felicity, than you should have gained possession of our woeful father's lands: for as if God had prospered him, you should have inherited his honors and manors, so if you apply diligently this book, seeking to direct your life according to the rule of the same, you shall be an inheritor of such riches, as neither the covetous shall withdraw from you, neither the thief shall steal, neither yet the moths corrupt: desire with David, my best sister, to understand the law of the Lord your God, live still to die, that you by death may purchase eternal life, and trust not that the tenderness of your age shall lengthen your life: for unto God, when he calleth, all hours, times and seasons are alike, and blessed are they whose lamps are furnished when he cometh, for as soon will the Lord be glorified in the young as in the old.

My good sister, once more again let me entreat thee to learn to die: deny the world, defy the devil, and despise the flesh, and delight yourself only in the Lord: be penitent for your sins, and yet despair not: be strong in faith, yet presume not; and desire with St. Paul to be dissolved and to be with Christ, with whom, even in death there is life.

Be like the good servant, and even at midnight be waking, lest when death cometh and stealeth upon you, like a thief in the night, you be with the servants of darkness found sleeping; and lest for lack of oil you be found like the five foolish virgins, or like him that had not on the wedding garment, and then you be cast into darkness, or banished from the marriage: rejoice in Christ, as I trust you do, and seeing you have the name of a Christian, as near as you can follow the steps, and be a true imitator of your master Christ Jesus, and take up your cross, lay your sins on his back, and always embrace him.

Now as touching my death, rejoice as I do my dearest sister, that I shall be delivered of this corruption, and put on incorruption: for I am assured that I shall, for losing of a mortal life, win one that is immortal, joyful, and everlasting: the which I pray God grant you in his most blessed hour, and send you his all-saving grace to live in his fear, and to die in the true Christian faith: from which in God's name I exhort you that you never swerve, neither through hope of life, nor fear of death: for if you will deny his truth to give length to a weary and corrupt breath, God himself will deny you, and by vengeance make short what you by your soul's loss would prolong: but if you will cleave to him, he will stretch

131

forth your days to an uncircumscribed comfort, and to his own glory: to the which glory, God bring me now and you hereafter, when it shall please him to call you. Farewell once again, my beloved sister, and put your only trust in God, who only must help you. Amen.

Your loving sister,
Jane Dudley [Pearson 133].

Lady Jane then wrote her sister one last time.

The last awful scene, my ever dear Catherine approaches! Pray for the constancy of your sister; pray that she may never lose sight of the glorious crown awaiting her in the presence of her Redeemer! — That she may not be induced by weakness or fear, in the last trying moment, to accept of the Queen's offers of pardon, at the price of her immortal hopes.

What is this life, so full of woe and vicissitude, that we should purchase it, or any of its enjoyments, by aught that is base and unworthy?

Adhere, my Catherine, to the practice of virtue, and may thy sister be enabled, by her example, to animate thee to persevere steadily in thy holy faith, to the latest moment of thy existence.

May the present I send thee, in a still more forcible manner, excite thy soul to constancy in that divine religion, in defense of which so many saints and martyrs have resigned their lives.

You will trace in many places of this sacred book, the well-known writings of your Jane. May the remarks which she has at different times noted in it, be of use to you, to strengthen your faith and hope; and when your sister is laid low and silent in the dust, may she yet assist and guide you by her precepts.

I have been summoning up all my fortitude, to support the much dreaded separation from friends so dear to me! affectionate parents! amiable and beloved husband, whose grief and tenderness melts my very soul! and a sister and cousin, dear to my heart!

My father's grief and remorse also penetrates my soul most sensibly. I have been endeavoring to reason with them. I have used that best of all arguments, fully convincing and satisfying to myself, that we are separating but for a moment, to reunite eternally in a state where all is light and liberty, and love; and where our happiness will never have an end!

Let this, my sweet Catherine, be your consolation also, and let it excite your warmest endeavors to become possessor of so glorious a prize.

Take care of your amending health, lest a relapse be the consequence of too severe a sorrow for your Jane.

If my friends with me do undergo the approaching doom, in a manner that will not disgrace them, let them not discompose the steadiness of my mind, by violence of grief — for the pangs of parting will be the greatest I shall feel.

Farewell, my dearest sister, remember in your prayers, and forgive the errors of your

Jane [Lane, Vol. II 98].

On February 12, the appointed hour arrived. The officer of the Tower called them forth, and "they met the summons with a temper that shew's a solemn serious sense of death, mix'd with a noble scorn to all its terrors" (Bayley 433).

Many solemn and moving accounts of the day have filled numerous books, but the unembellished facts are moving enough. Guildford was executed first on Tower-Hill, and then Jane. The lieutenant of the Tower led her to the scaffold, attended by Mistress Tylney and Mistress Ellen, her servants, and Master Feckenham. From the platform, she recited a short speech she had prepared for the occasion.

Good people, I come hither to die. And by a law I am condemned to the same: the fact indeed against the Queens Highness was unlawful and consenting there unto by me. But touching the procurement and desire thereof by me on my behalf I do wash my hands thereof in innocence, before God and the face of you good Christian people this day. I pray you all good Christian people to bear me witness that I die a true Christian woman and that I look to be saved by none other means but only by the mercy of God. In the merits of the blood of his only son Jesus Christ, and I confess when I did know the word of God, I neglected the same and loved myself and the world and therefore this plague of punishment is happily and worthily happened unto me for my sins. And yet I thank God of his goodness that he has thus given me a time and respite to repent: and now good people while I am alive I pray you to assist me with your prayers [Brown 79].

After reciting the above, she knelt down to pray and asked Master Feckenham, "Shall I say this psalm?" He replied, "Yes," and she repeated in English the psalm *Miserere Mei, Deus.* She then said to Feckenham, "God will requite you, good sir, for your humanity, though your discourses gave me more uneasiness than all the terrors of my approaching death."

Bayley goes on,

> Having finished her devotions the Lady Jane began to prepare for the last scene of the mournful tragedy. She removed her gloves and handkerchief then gave them to her maiden, Mrs. Ellen, and her book to Master Brydges, the lieutenant's brother; and, as she began to untie her gown, the executioner proceeded to assist her, but she requested him to let her alone, and turned to her two gentlewomen, who helped her off therewith, giving her a fair handkerchief to bind about her eyes. Then the executioner, on his knees, begged her forgiveness, which she granted most willingly, begging him to dispatch her quickly. Kneeling down on some straw which covered the platform, she turned again to the executioner saying, "will you take it off before I lay me down?" he answered, "No, madam." She then tied the handkerchief over her eyes, and feeling anxiously for the block, said, "What shall I do? Where is it, where is it?" when one of the by-standers directed her to the fatal instrument, on which she laid her neck, and most patiently, Christianly, and constantly, yielded to God her soul, exclaiming, "Lord, into thy hands I commend my spirit" [Bayley 435].

The following is a description of the days that followed the execution; it comes from the *Historical Memorials, Ecclesiastical and Civil, of events under the reign of Queen Mary I,* by John Strype from a 1721 edition.

> Thus this Black Monday began, with the Execution of this most Noble and Virtuous Lady and her Husband. On the same day, for a terrifying Sight, were many new Pairs of Gallows set up in London. As at every Gate one, two pair in Cheapside, one in Fleetstreet, one in Smithfield, one in Holborn, one at Leadenhall, one at St. Magnus, one at Billingsgate, one at Pepper Alley Gate,

one at St. George's, one in Barnsby Street, one on Tower Hill, one at Charing Cross, and one at Hide Park Corner. These gallows remained standing until Wednesday when men were hanged on every Gibbet, and some quartered also. In Cheapside six; at Aldgate one, hanged and quartered; at Leadenhall three; at Bishopgate one, and was quartered; at Moorgate one, and he was quartered; at Ludgate one and he was quartered; at Billingsgate three hanged; at St. Magnus three hanged; at Tower Hill three hanged; at Holborn three hanged; at Fleetstreet three hanged; at Paul's Churchyard four; at Pepper Alley Corner three; at Barneby Street three; at St. George's three; at Charing Cross four; whereof two belonged to the Court; at Hidepark Corner three, one of them named Pollard, a water bearer. Those three were hanged in chains. But seven were quartered, and their bodies and heads set upon the gates of London.

And that is how Mary earned the nickname of "Bloody Mary."

Within days of Jane's execution, Lady Anne conveyed her great loss in a letter to Lady Laurana, including an interesting account of Jane's execution by an unknown gentleman.

Alas, my Laurana! — The awful scene is past! the curtain is drawn! the tragedy is concluded! and yet I live! yet wear a miserable existence, that affords no hope of happiness! But do you expect that I can give you any account of the horrid wreck of all that was dearest to me on earth? — For a fortnight past, the violence of my agitation has confined me to my bed in a fever; my life, for some days, was despaired of.

Merciful Heaven! Why did not my heart burst, when I saw that white neck meekly laid on the block, like a lamb under the murderous knife! — But I saw no more; I was, in pity, deprived of my senses at that heart-rendering sight. — If you will pardon me, I will transmit to you the relation of the sorrowful scene, writ and authenticated by a gentleman; which will I am certain, draw tears of sorrowful sensibility from your gentle soul, though a Catholic.

The Duke of Norfolk, and my uncle, Lord Thomas Grey, have also suffered. — My father has not yet appeared; God grant he may be in safety.

Lady Catherine came to town, on receiving my last letter to her, in the hope of seeing her excellent sister once more; but she came too late. — The poor mother and sister are inconsolable; the latter still ill. I have not yet seen them: I cannot see them: not can I, at present, write any more. Farewell,

Anne Grey.

Here follows the gentleman's account.

On the day of Lady Jane's execution, her husband desired to see her, but she refused her consent, and informed him, that the tenderness of their parting would overcome the fortitude of both; and too much unbend their minds from that constancy, which their approaching end required of them. Their separation, she said, would be only for a moment; and they would soon rejoin each other in a scene, where their affections would be for ever reunited; and where death, disappointment, and misfortunes, could no longer have access to them, to disturb their eternal felicity.

It had been intended to execute Lady Jane and Lord Guildford together, on the same scaffold, at Tower-Hill; but the council, dreading the compassion of the people, for their youth, beauty, innocence, and noble birth, changed their orders, and gave directions that she should be beheaded within the verge of the Tower.

She saw her husband led to execution; and having given him, from the window, some token of her remembrance, she waited, with composure, till her own appointed hour should bring her to the like fate. She even saw his headless body carried back, and found herself more confirmed by the reports she heard of the constancy of his end, than shaken by so tender and melancholy a spectacle.

Sir John Gage, the constable of the Tower, when he led her to execution, desired her to bestow on him some small present, which he might keep as a perpetual memorial of her. She gave him her table-book, on which she had just written three sentences, on seeing her husband's dead body; one in Greek, another in Latin, and third in English. The purport of them was, that human justice was against his body, but that divine mercy would be favorable to his soul. That if her fault desired punishment, her youth, at least, and her inexperience, were worthy of excuse; and that God, and posterity, she trusted, would show her favor.

On the scaffold, she made a speech to the by-standers; in which the mildness of her disposition, led her to take the blame wholly on herself, without uttering one complaint on the severity with which she had been treated.

She said, her offense was not her having laid her hand on the crown, but the not rejecting it with sufficient constancy; that she had less erred through ambition, than through reverence for her parents, whom she had been taught to respect and obey; that she willingly received death, as the only satisfaction she could make to the injured state; and though her infringement of the laws had been constrained, she would show, by her voluntary submission to their sentence, that she was desirous to atone for that disobedience into which too much filial pity had betrayed her; that she had justly deserved this punishment for being made the instrument, though the unwilling instrument, of the ambition of others; that the story of her life, she hoped, might at least be useful; by proving, that innocence excuses not great errors, if they tend any-wise to the destruction of the common-wealth.

After uttering these words, she caused herself to be disrobed by her women, and with a steady, and serene countenance, submitted herself to the executioner. [Lane, Vol. II 104].

***

Here, perhaps some would conclude the story, now that the main character is dead, but several letters remain from the "Lane letters." They paint a vivid portrait of the turbulence in Tudor England with Mary on the throne. As an indication of just how unsettled the period was, an estimate of between seventy-one and ninety executions took place at the time of Jane's execution. Henry Machyn, an undertaker, listed forty-five executions on February 14 alone. Around 480 were convicted in all, though not every one of them was executed.

Lady Anne conveys those very images in a letter to Lady Laurana, shortly after Jane's execution.

My soul, almost annihilated within me, seems convinced that nothing in life can ever again excite either animated hopes or fears, or engage those passions which fan the flame of human life, and contribute to its existence.

Dead, like the season of the year, are my hopes! the summer, indeed, will return — the stormy winds subside — the trees renew their verdure, though defaced by the wintry frost. — But when will my lovely Jane revive? — When will those fair frames, now moldering in the cold grave, spring up a-new, and re-appear to gladden and delight me? — When shall I again behold them, hand in hand, with animated and striking countenances, enter my apartment, and summon me to some rural walk, or pleasing amusement? while I contemplate their mutual affection with exquisite delight, and, sharing the friendship of each partake of their felicity!

Alas, it is all over! — an horrible chasm intervenes! — The dull gloom of unavailing sorrow succeeds, and possess my whole soul! — No comfort can I afford the poor deserted wife and mother — I dread to see them, and would willingly shut myself here in my apartment, never more to leave it.

The light of sun is even hateful to me, though its radiance is enfeebled by the clouds of winter, and every thing the world call great and beautiful, is, in my opinion, insipid, foolish, or vain! — Kings and Queens are either pageants of a day, almost equally vain with the gaudy insect which sports in the summer fervent ray, and then vanishes into dust; or tyrants that enslave and destroy their country. Even books and study, what are they without a friend and companion, with whom to share their pleasures? — Alas, just such a one I once had! but she is no more, she is gone for ever! — she lies low in the ground, and the dust covers her!

(continuation)

I have been conveyed to Lord Herbert's, where the Duchess now is. I cannot describe our interview. All our past aching feelings are renewed, and Lady Catherine is too ill to support the conflicts of her tender and gentle soul; I fear she will not long remain on earth.

To heighten the picture of woe, the Queen is not yet satiated with blood.

She has filled the Tower, and all the prisons, with Nobility and Gentry, whom their interest with the nation, rather than any appearance of guilt, had made the objects of her suspicions.

Among the rest, the Duchess of Suffolk and her daughter, and Lord Herbert, are ordered to prepare for a residence in the Tower, during her Majesty's pleasure.

They are to be conveyed there tomorrow, which short interval it was with difficulty they obtained, to prepare for a mansion, whence they may never again depart, but to be conveyed to a much smaller one in the grave!

You may imagine their horror and grief, to be sent to the very place, which has so recently been the scene of execution to friends so dear to them!

My sorrow, I believe, equaled theirs; it was such as left me little ability of consoling them.

I promised to see them frequently, if permitted — painful as it would be to enter again that place of blood; and I remained with them as long as I possibly could — since to converse, even in all the agony of grief, with a sharer in that grief, is a relief to the wounded heart, and we separated more resigned than we met.

Religious consolations, forgot in the first violence of our terror, came to the aid of each, in endeavoring to impart them to the others, and began to soften a little the deep impression, which the late shocking events had created on our hearts.

They have since, by slow degrees, had more and more ascendancy over my mind, so much so, that I have been enabled to visit my unhappy friends in the Tower several times.

When, however, I first entered within those walls, my heart sunk within me; I could scarcely keep myself from fainting, and with difficulty my attendants supported me to the prison of the unhappy mother and her children, which was that of the once martyred, but now blessed Jane.

Ah, cruel Mary, said I, as I entered, is not thy cup of vengeance full! Wilt thou never forget thy malice to the family of Suffolk! — that thou thus places them in the very scene where the excellent daughter suffered! even in the very prison in which she was immured! — Must not their regrets be perpetual, unalleviated by any change of scene or society? — O when will thy doom fall on me also? — It would be some consolation to remain here with my amiable friends, it is a place which suits my gloomy soul.

Yet, my Laurana, painful as it was to visit in such a situation those dear friends, which forced from my soul those bitter complaints — our frequent conversations with each other have afforded us consolation and fortitude.

Our subject the virtues of our deceased friends, point our views to that world of happiness to which they are ascended.

I now long for a state more felicitous — where no tyrants reign — and where again I shall behold my Jane.

Edward's image presents itself to my fancy, and increases my desire of entering that passage, which will conduct me to realms of everlasting light and bliss! — bliss for ever shed from me on earth, and which, possessed by the most happy mortals on its surface, when compared with the joys of the blessed, is only like a transient meteor, flashing over the light for a moment, and the steady, cheerful, and invigorating light of the noon-day sun.

The virtues of my Jane, and that excellent Prince, are now rewarded with eternal crowns, and never fading honors!

How happy was I in their society in my childish days, before thoughtless delight was destroyed by the keen edge of disappointment! It is the experience of past sorrows, that plants stings in every comfort we possess, and anticipates to our minds uncertain ills.

But in that future land of pleasure, delight is ever springing anew in the heart; and virtuous friendship began on earth, will be a source of endless and increasing joy.

The foundation of life and happiness will admit us into his blissful presence, — and in his presence is fullness of joy; and at his right hand are pleasures forever more!

Blessed state! let my God call me home whenever he pleases — or, which is to me far more difficult to say, let him keep me here as long as he pleases. Life at the longest is short.

Let me pray that resignation may smooth my way, and let my endeavors to acquire this most arduous task, employ the remainder of my days.

Adieu,

My dear Laurana,

Anne Grey [Lane, Vol. II 114].

If Lady Anne's portrayal of the dreadful events unfolding in England is dramatic, the reply from Lady Laurana, still in a convent in Florence, is also dramatic. She has converted to Protestantism.

How feelingly, my dear Lady Anne, have you related the past horrid and affecting event! — In what animated forms described your anguish! — And with what sympathy has my heart borne its testimony of sorrow to every tale of woe, as you proceeded! — The circumstances alone are such, indeed, as must excite pity and admiration in every breast not wholly callous.

Blessed martyrs! — Excellent, noble Jane! — I almost envy thy fate! — Happy Lord Guildford too! — United again to thy fair partner: never more to feel the pangs of separation, and the sorrows of absence. United to her in a state, beyond expression blessed.

I am become a convert to thy reformed principles, and abhor persecution, with the other errors of popery, with sincere conviction.

I have a sensible acquaintance here, my dear friend, who is a Protestant; and who has satisfied some of my doubts, in a relation of my mother's, to whom, sister Clara has introduced me, and who has invited me frequently to her house. There I sometimes meet Protestant divines, whose arguments have assisted my conversion.

But what, beyond all this, worked the change, was an English Bible which was lent me; which language, though not my parents, is mine, as I was born in England, and understand it equally with Italian. Almost every chapter in it, strikes conviction into my understanding, and the light of truth into my heart.

My zeal is now so great in favor of my newly acquired faith, that, I think, I should rejoice to be a martyr in its cause. Yet, let me not be too secure; zeal, frequently indiscrete zeal, is the concomitant of new opinions: may mine be moderated by charity, by toleration, by every gentle and humane consideration, which becomes frail and erring creatures to their fellow-beings, be they of what religion they may.

God, who is the author of being, and the former of the human heart, has implanted in every one those sentiments, from climate, constitution, and education, which will best answer the purpose of his providential dispensations. Blest, thrice blest are those, who enjoy the benefit of the Christian revelation! are enabled to distinguish the light of truth! and enjoy the privileges of such a Gospel! — But those are happy only as their practice conforms with their principles, and who meekly, and with simplicity, receive the precepts of the Gospel, and obey them.

I am rejoiced, my dear Lady Anne, that you have a little recovered your mind from the first shock of your recent misfortunes.

Lady Jane's fortitude, and your resignation, are both the happy effects of your divine principles. — Ah! that I could attain this perfection! — But I must acknowledge, that it is with great difficulty, I can support my too keen apprehensions, concerning the fate of the amiable Earl of Devonshire. I tremble to open your letters, lest they should contain some dreadful account of his fate.

That impetuous temper, which is natural to me, will not always be controlled; and I am quite ashamed to own, that I am almost distracted by my fears on this account.

I think, I see him condemned by the cruel Mary to horrid tortures! I feel his agonies! And am almost resolved to destroy myself by poison, rather than suffer such acute misery! but, on a sudden, a divine ray from Heaven illuminates my benighted soul! I am feelingly awake to my guilt and danger; supplicate the mercy of the Deity; and again experience that composure, that hope, that resignation, which sincere contrition, is fitted to obtain.

Pity thy poor friend, my dear Lady Anne, and teach me to support, with steadiness, whatever misfortunes are decreed by Heaven to your

Laurana [Lane, Vol. II 128].

Among the letters William Lane included in his 1791 edition, the next — written in middle to late April 1554 — warrants a book in itself.

On March 15, Thomas Wyatt was tried and convicted for his part in a conspiracy with "the object of seizing the Tower and levying war against the Queen to deprive her of her royal title." He was executed on April 11, 1554.

History has not recorded the fate of Lady Anne's father, John Grey. Both her uncles, Henry and Thomas, were executed. Lady Anne masked her father's location in France, using only a first letter to indicate the name of the place.

I was sitting one evening in my solitary apartment, in that kind of composed melancholy, which is cherished by those who have experienced deep afflictions, and which, so far from corroding the heart, softens it to benevolence and compassion, when a servant came to say, that a gentleman wanted to impart something of importance to me, and requested he might speak to me alone; I was surprised at the message, and hesitated, at first, if I had best comply with his request or not; however, I soon admitted him, and how still more surprised and delighted was I, to receive a letter from my father, who writ me, that he had found a safe retreat, at the time that my uncle Suffolk's party was obliged to disperse and hide themselves, and that he remained in it till the search of the Queen's troops was over; that then, by the disguise of a common sailor, he obtained a passage to France, where he then was, and meant to remain, till some happy revolution rendered his country more safe to him.

My father added, that he wanted the consolations of his beloved daughter's company, and was in daily apprehensions for her safety; while she remained in England; he therefore entreated me to commit myself to the care of the gentleman, who was the barer of his letter, and who would convey me safely to him, having a proper disguise, to prevent my being discovered.

Rejoiced as I was, to recover a father whom I had almost given up for lost, my thoughts, from this pleasing circumstance, reverted to my unfortunate friends in the Tower, whom I felt great regret to quit.

I, however, told the gentleman, I was greatly rejoiced to hear of my father's safety, and would prepare myself to attend him in two days. He respectfully urged me to set out immediately, lest it should, by any means, reach the Queen's ears, that my father had sent for me.

I told him, he need be under no apprehension, but that, if possible, I would go sooner: as the Queen had confiscated all the houses and estates of my father, I had been in a friend's house ever since the late troubles; I had therefore very little to take with me, besides some valuable jewels of my mother's and my own.

As soon as my father's messenger was gone, I was preparing myself to visit my friends in the Tower, and to take a final leave of them, which was a task almost too much for my resolution, when, who should I see enter my apartment, but the Earl of Devonshire.

On hearing his voice, I started from my reveries; yet, like one just awakened from a troublesome dream, could not believe my senses; nor that what I saw was real.

He at last convinced me it was himself, and told me, that the Queen's marriage, which I imagine you must have heard of, had occasioned his enlargement, from motives which he could not account for, unless it was the wish of popularity; Don Philip had set him at liberty.

We spent two or three hours together, in the painfully-pleasing employment, of conversing on the late melancholy fate of our friends; mixing joy with our tears, that they were now at liberty from Mary's tyranny, their parent's ambition, and all the ills that beset this mortal life.

He, almost at his entrance, asked impatiently if I had heard from you, whom he has so long been utterly excluded from by his confinement, as well as from writing to you.

You will not, I am sure, be angry, if I own I read some parts of your letters to him: he was delighted with them, lamented his hard fate, in being so long separated from you, and said, he was at length permitted to go abroad, as he has obtained the Queen's consent; that he would immediately go to Florence as he was impatient to see you, and as he would make you the offer of his hand; and, if you would consent to marry him, he would reside abroad, till it was more safe for him to reside in his own country.

I entreated him to give me some account of the reasons, that led Mary to suspect him of a passion for Elizabeth, and of their mutually conspiring against her. He said, he would relate the few incidents which had happened to him, since he parted from his dear Lady Laurana, and the unfortunate Lady Jane, at the Tower, which I will give you, as nearly as I can, in his own words.

"When I first came out into the world, and was introduced, by the Queen, to the young nobility at court, I felt so conscious of my want of those accomplishments suited to my rank, and which, the many years I had been immured in prison, had prevented my acquiring, that I was resolved to devote as much of my time as I could to attain them; in the mean time, the Queen's partiality for me, would not suffer me to enjoy so much retirement as I wished for, for that purpose, and which also my long habits of solitary life had rendered almost necessary to me; as well as my love for Lady Laurana, and my earnest desire to form myself, by my address and manners, more worthy of her.

"The reception I met with at Court, however, was too insinuating for a young man, who had been secluded so long from society.

"Not to have many charms, and the only thing that rendered it irksome to me, was my absence from Laurana, and the Queen's passion, which I both dreaded and detested, and which she had very early, after our first acquaintance, got me informed of.

"Her jealously of the Lady Elizabeth, also, who is an amiable Princess, had given me frequent cause of uneasiness; for her conversation, both engaging and instructive to a man like me, who has had so few opportunities of conversing with sensible and well-bred women, had induced me to attach myself a good deal to her, particularly as she showed me great attention.

"The Queen you know hates the Princess, and could not support the idea that I should slight her passion, and devote my time to her sister.

"In vain I assured her, on my honor, that I had never made the slightest effort to gain the Princess's affection.

"She could not believe that I would refuse her hand and crown, without the prospect of an equivalent at some future period.

144

"I entreated her Majesty to permit me to go abroad; expressed my earnest desire to see foreign courts, and to get a knowledge of the customs and manners of other nations, but she would by no means consent to it.

"As I generally informed Elizabeth of the Queen's threats concerning her, she thought it best to retire from court into the country, as she met with every instance of disrespect, that the Queen could show her in public.

"And not long after Wyatt's insurrection (which has been so fatal to the Duke of Suffolk's family) commenced, Elizabeth and myself were accused of being concerned in it, and both committed to different prisons.

"But as Wyatt, on his execution, entirely acquitted us of having the least concern in it, the Lady Elizabeth was tried by the Council, and vindicated her innocence so well, that the Queen was obliged to release her from confinement, as well as myself; at that time, more from the fear of the people than inclination.

"For she soon found another pretence of confining her again, which was by proposing an alliance for her with the Duke of Savoy; which, however, that Princess, in a submissive manner, begged leave to decline, saying, she wished to remain single. But this was construed into a confirmation of an engagement with me; and, in the resistance she made to her Majesty's pleasure, she found as she thought, a sufficient plea to confine her to Woodstock, and to send me to Fotheringay Castle.

"Here we remained till the Queen's marriage with Don Philip, and his affection for popularity induced him to release those of the Nobility which Mary had confined on suspicion, amongst the rest myself, and also to undertake the defense of the Princess Elizabeth from the malice of her sister.

"He, therefore, sat her at liberty, much to the disgust of the Queen, who, I believe, already perceives that Philip is more influenced by ambitious views than love to her.

"The Princess has not, however, since been at Court, but I received a message from her, soon after our enlargement, requesting to speak with me.

"I immediately visited her, and we met with expressions of that friendship, which a similarity of sentiments and dispositions had united us in.

"She told me, she had continually regretted that the Queen's unjust suspicions of me, on her account, should have been so injurious to me; and that she would willingly undertake any thing that might contribute to my happiness, and should rejoice to make any compensation for my past sufferings on her account. She said, there was something in my manner at times, which convinced her that some Lady had possession of my affections, though I dare not own it, on account of the Queen's partiality for me; but now her Majesty was married, she thought she had influence enough with Philip to engage him to promote the alliance; she, therefore besought me to consider her as my sincere friend, and to unfold to her my inclinations without reserve.

"I was struck with her goodness, but yet was at a loss what to do. Elizabeth, though possessed of eminent virtues, is vain, and fond of admiration.

"I had, on many occasions, observed, that she did not like that any Lady should have the preference to herself, not only in mine, but in the opinion of those Lords about her, whom she favored with any marks of attention.

"I thought too, that there was something in her manner con-fused, and as if she meant, by an appearance of generosity, to draw me into a declaration of particular attachment to herself; and if so, instead of extricating myself from the difficulties that lay in my way to the possession of Laurana, by my confidence in the Prin-cess, I should only, perhaps, be involving myself in greater.

"What could I do? I had not seen enough of courts, and the deceits of them, to submit to the meanness of a lie. I was silent and confused; it was some time, before I could recollect myself suffi-ciently to thank her, for the interest she took in my happiness; to beg she would not urge me on a subject which I must ever be silent on, and to assure her, that the sense of her goodness would never be erased from my heart; and that, wherever my fate drove me, the Princess Elizabeth would ever possess the most sincere friendship of Devonshire.

"The Princess blushed, and I perceived that this speech flat-tered her vanity; she evidently imputed my confusion and reserve, to a passion for herself, which my respect for her, and the situation we were in, forbade my revealing.

"I was rejoiced, therefore, that I had not revealed my secret; and she did not urge me any more on the subject, but desired me to inform her if, in any thing, she could be serviceable to me with Don Philip.

"I told her, I thought myself very insecure in England, in my present situation, and had also a wish to improve myself by travel, and, if she would have the goodness to desire Don Philip to intercede with the Queen for that purpose, I should esteem myself infinitely obliged to her, though I should still regret the loss of her conversation, which had afforded me so many agreeable hours.

"The Princess took my compliment graciously, and promised to endeavor to obtain my desire, which she soon after effected.

"I went to court, to thank the Queen for this permission, but she would not see me, which I was not otherwise concerned at, than as it may affect the Princess's safety. I have seen Lady Elizabeth several times since, who has always shown me great attention, and friendly solicitude for my welfare.

"I am ready now to set out, and will, with pleasure, convey whatever letters, or message, you may have to your friend, my charming Laurana: the impatience which I suffer to behold her again cannot be equaled."

I informed the Earl, when he had ended his account, that my father was in safety, in France, and desired me to join him there; that he had sent a messenger to convey me to him, and that I should set out in two days.

He seemed quite rejoiced at the event; he said he would prepare himself to accompany me, and that when he had obtained his Laurana's hand, he would endeavor to prevail on her, to make mine the place of their residence.

Then, added he, I may hope for an amiable female companion for my wife, which will contribute to her happiness, and with *still* so many worthy friends about us, may I not flatter myself that, in spite of the past cruelty of my fate, I shall be one of the happiest of mortals?

I objected to his accompanying me as highly improper, since it would lay open my father's situation, and our affairs to the inspection of the Queen, in all probability; that he would go abroad in a manner suitable to his rank, but that I had a disguise provided for me, and should go in the most private manner that was possible.

He said, he could not prevail on himself to permit me to go, attended only by a stranger; that therefore, if I would pardon him, he would recommend to me to go in disguise, and attended by this gentleman, in his train, or, as passengers in the same vessel; that as soon as they were landed on the French shore, he would privately attend me, and commit me in safety to my father's arms.

I thanked him very sincerely, and said, I had no objection to his proposal, but the apprehension, least he should render himself liable to the Queen's displeasure, should we be discovered; or that, my father's asylum being found out, the consequences might be fatal to him; and those fears, I owned, were so great, that I should not enjoy a moment's peace during my voyage. I therefore declined his offer, and determined in the disguise prepared for me, and under the protection of the gentleman my father had sent, to commit myself to Providence, and take my voyage.

I went and took a sorrowful leave of my friends in the Tower, who expressed a great and generous pleasure in my father's safety, notwithstanding their own sad fate, and prayed that I might safely join my father.

They also found pleasure in the Earl's release, and prospect of happiness, and discovered those great and worthy minds, which, though under the chastening hand of Heaven themselves, can rejoice without envy at the felicity of their friends and fellow creatures.

Long we lingered before we could think of parting, and nothing but the approach of night could tear me from them; and, even then, I thought, was I to consult my own inclination, I had rather, at the time, have remained with them to console and entertain them, than forsake them in so bitter a fate. — But my father's will, and his want of an affectionate daughter, to render his exile more tolerable, enabled me to make a violent effort of resolution, and quit the place.

But adieu — perhaps forever! I could not say!

No sleep scarcely had I that night, but wept almost incessantly.

My father's messenger appeared in the morning, and brought with him my disguise — I told him I should be ready to attend him in the evening, and desired him to prepare every thing for me, and return early.

I had taken leave of my friend, in whose house I was, and was preparing to depart, when I was surprised by the appearance of the Earl, completely disguised as well as myself; who said he could not suffer me to set out without his protection; that, therefore, he had given orders that his suit should go in the vessel they were designed for, and told them and the captain, that he was obliged himself to sail in another ship.

Though much alarmed for his safety, he would hear none of my objections, and we went on board of the vessel provided for me.

As soon as we had sat down in the cabin, the Earl entered into an agreeable conversation, which a little dissipated my melancholy thoughts at quitting England, perhaps for ever, that recent scene of so much bloodshed, and so many horrors; but it was the

148

recollection of my unhappy friends, that rendered my heart heavy; nor could I banish them from my idea, for in spite of his endeavors to awaken more pleasing and cheerful remembrances, our conversation adverted to them.

Yet, he still encouraged me to hope, that they would soon be released; that it would be of no consequence to the Queen to keep them confined, since their party was quelled entirely. He entreated me, therefore, to endeavor to banish sorrow from my heart, and to sympathize with him in his extreme joy, at the thoughts of seeing again his charming Lady Laurana.

I told him, I would endeavor to do it, in the hopes he had given me, that my captive friends would soon be at liberty. I began to look forward also, as the shore of France approached, to the pleasure of seeing again a father, for whom I had the sincerest duty and affection, preserved from the wreck of fate. I felt the most affecting gratitude to Heaven, for this consolation in my heavy afflictions; and for that goodness, which had not suffered me to sink under them, but preserved me to assist in supporting and comforting my exiled father.

Thus, I am persuaded, will all those, who listen to the divine lessons of resignation in their sorrows, have reason for gratitude in the midst of the severest fate; even though they cannot penetrate the veil of Providence, nor understand why they are thus severely dealt with.

I had began this letter before I received yours, which both delighted and shocked me. I was charmed to think that you had abjured the errors of popery; admired your sentiments on zeal and charity; but how was I shocked at the account of your impatience at the confinement of the Earl! — May Heaven preserve the reason of my friend, exclaimed I, with fervor! — O! may she be preserved from destroying herself! — from abruptly presenting a guilty soul, stained with suicide, before a pure and righteous God! — O! lay not on her more than her frail nature can support!

I congratulate you, my fair friend, on the happiness that awaits you. — Write to me at B-, where my father is. — I send this from the first inn we put up at in France. We remain here to-night, and in the morning, proceed on our journey to B-.

The Earl is resolved to accompany me; my father will rejoice to see him: his own ship and suite are not yet arrived; he has only one servant with him, in whom he can confide. — My father intends to meet me half way. With what delight shall I see him again, after so long an absence?

Farewell, my charming Laurana; you have with this a letter from the Earl.

Anne Grey [Lane 136].

The next letter is a short continuation of the previous letter.

I found my father at the place he appointed to meet me, in per-fect health. He received me with every testimony of extreme joy — yet a moment after, it was suddenly checked by the bitter recollec-tion of all we and our friends had suffered since our separation. We offered the tribute of a few tears to the memory of the marty-red pair.

When my father, resuming his composure, expressed again his joy at seeing me, and declared, that in respect to his own share in the late calamities, he had already forgot all his past sorrows in his present happiness.

Judge, my dear Laurana, what pleasure I received from this information, and if I was not again reconciled to life — since I was become of so much consequence to the felicity of the best of par-ents.

The Earl partook of my joy, as my father did in his approaching happiness, and we retired to our apartments with those pleasing impressions on our hearts, which usually procure sweet and sound repose.

We cannot prevail with the Earl to remain more than one day with us — to-morrow he sets out, and with him this letter, which, therefore, I have not time to lengthen.

May no ill accident impede his speedy arrival at Florence, and may all happiness attend him and my fair friend, prays her

Anne Grey [Lane, Vol. II 172].

Lady Laurana wrote the following letter to Lady Anne in late May or early June. Lady Laurana and Edward Courtenay were married about that time. The numerous though brief accounts that remain of Edward Courtenay do not mention his marriage to anyone. Perhaps they succeeded in keeping their secret.

With greater joy than I can express, I beheld again my amiable Devonshire, improved in person and manners, and blest with a heart noble, generous, and sincere; such a heart as Queens have been proud to have called their own.

About a month after his arrival we were married; but how unworthy do I esteem myself of such a treasure?

I have informed him of the change you were the first means of causing in my religious sentiments. His opinion[s] very nearly coincide with mine, and our happiness is more complete on this account; indeed it is impossible for any woman to possess a more tender and affectionate husband, and I only wish for the presence of my dear Lady Anne to crown my felicity, and to see her united to a man equally amiable with the Earl of Devonshire.

Flatter me with the hopes of your company before the year is at an end, and be assured that my own happiness has not rendered me selfish, but that I have a heart, as open to all the feelings of friendly sympathy as ever.

I was charmed at the account the Earl gave me of your interview with your father; how happy am I that you are safe under his protection, and out of the reach of the resentful Mary. But shall I own, that I sometimes have apprehensions invade my mind, lest her malice should snatch my husband from me.

No one knows the secret of our marriage, but the relation of my mother's, whom I mentioned, and at whose house I live, whose disposition is too amiable to doubt her fidelity; sister Clara, whom I parted from with regret, and our two confidential servants.

The Earl has a house of his own, where his servants are, but you may imagine, the greatest part of his time he passes with me; thus has he guarded against a discovery: but the uncertainty of all earthly happiness, cannot but check our transports, and ought not allow of too great an elation of mind, which is inconsistent with our state of trial, and would attach us too much to the world, and draw us off from our pursuit of a better.

The Earl joins with me in every good wish to your father and yourself.

Adieu.

Laurana [Lane 176].

The tone of the next letter from Lady Anne to Lady Laurana reflects the calm returning to her life, removed from the horrors and despair of England.

With the sincerest joy, I congratulate my friends on their marriage! — May every blessing attend you both! and may Providence continue your bliss for many, many years!

Let not your fears of the future, render you ungrateful for present joys, my fair friend. Providence, if it pleases, can cause such a change, even in Mary's heart, as may be productive of the restoration of your husband to his native country, with safety and peace.

At all events, though the vicissitude of mortal things ought to prevent a too great security in our minds, yet, the certainty of an over-ruling power of Infinite Wisdom and Goodness, leaves us room to hope, that our happiness will be finally promoted, and ought to inspire us with cheerfulness, hope, and gratitude.

I have had the pleasure of a letter from the Duchess of Suffolk. She informs me, that Lady Catherine's declining health, has induced the Queen, at her earnest petition, to consent to their enlargement, that her daughter may have the benefit of free air and exercise; on the condition that they live retired in the country. She expresses great sorrow at her daughter's ill health, mixed with resignation, should she lose her, and hopes of soon following her.

I feel my heart relieved from a heavy burden, at the information of their freedom; and yet a tender grief hangs over it, on account of the declining health of my young friend; whose gentle spirits have, doubtless, been unable to stem the torrent of affliction that came raging around her on every side. Silent and uncomplaining, it shook her fair fabric, and will, I fear, finally dissolve it.

How mournful a sight for the affectionate mother! whom, I think, I love as I should a mother, had I ever known one: has she not been to me a mother? I have, undoubtedly, seen her in error, from her ambitious views for her daughter; but in every other respect, she is truly amiable; and is there a mortal free from error? at some time or other of their lives, or in some peculiar circumstances; all discover it; and whoever seeks to establish himself as a perfect character in the eye of the world, not only falls infinitely short of perfection, but degenerates into guilt; for he is tainted with arrogance and deceit.

I find that Lady Dudley is to reside with the Duchess; she has been with a friend, as I have, since the late confiscation of her husband's estates: she is a very worthy woman, and they will be a consolation to each other.

My father bids me to request that you will come and visit us very soon, which he thinks much more safe, both for your husband

and himself, than our visit to you would be; and, as the Earl has no connections to confine him where he is, or to any one place, let us meet here very soon. — I trust you will not refuse my request.

My father makes his to your husband with his own pen.

Adieu, Ever your,

Anne Grey [Lane 181].

In the next and final of the "Lane letters," Lady Laurana indicates to Lady Anne in the second paragraph why history has not recorded her marriage to Edward Courtenay.

With pleasure, my dear Lady Anne, we comply with your father's and your request, and are preparing to visit you very soon; the Earl only waits for letters from England: he means to take no English servant with him, besides the one whom he confides in; and I shall only have my woman, who is acquainted with our marriage.

We propose taking a house near your's, and remaining as long as circumstances of conveniency will admit. We mean to conceal our real names and quality, and to hire servants from the place you are at. This, I think, must elude Mary's vigilance; for, I assure you, we are liable to discovery here, from Mary's religion, and acquaintance with priests and cardinals: many of those residing here, the Earl knows, and as he has lately been rendered a conspicuous character, from the Queen's attention to him, these priests are too busy a set of beings, and too desirous to ingratiate themselves with her, not to give her so important a piece of information, as his marriage without her knowledge and consent. On the whole, therefore, it will be best for us to quit Florence on every account; though I regret leaving sister Clara, and the good Lady with whom I live, and considers me as her child.

We shall not wait for your reply, but set out as soon as possible. — You cannot imagine the pleasure I receive at the prospect of seeing you again, after so long an absence.

I rejoice that the Duchess of Suffolk is at liberty; God grant that Lady Catherine may be restored to her health.

Adieu, my dear friend, may our interview be a happy one.

Laurana [Lane, Vol. II 188].

CHAPTER 4. FURTHERMORE

The three items in this chapter are less central than those in the previous chapters. Lady Jane and Guildford reportedly exchanged three poems. Skeptical of their authenticity, this author has scrutinized them, and believes they deserve a place here, if only for the facts they contain.

The first two were transcribed from *Poems by Michael Drayton, Esquire. Newly corrected and augmented,* printed by William Stanby for John Smethwick, London, 1630. Drayton indicated on the title page that Lady Jane and Guildford exchanged the poems while they were prisoners in the Tower. The first begins with an argument, then the poem, composed by Jane Grey for Guildford Dudley. The piece concludes with a brief annotation by Drayton.

The second poem was composed by Dudley to the Lady Jane. An editor's note follows it as well. Words in italics are commented on by the editor at the end of each poem. This author's comments are in italics and parentheses.

The Lady Jane Gray
To the Lord Gilford Dudley

The Argument.

Edward the sixth timeless Life bereft;
(Though doubtfully) yet his dominion left
To his Sister Mary: but by Henry Grey,
Then Duke of Suffolk, bearing mighty sway,
With the Consent, and by the powerful hand.
Of John, the stout Duke of Northumberland,
His fourth son Gilford Dudley, they
To fair Jane Grey, which by the mother's side
Some Title claimed: this Marriage them between,
The Lady Jane was here proclaimed Queen.
But Mary soon prevailing by her power,
Cause those two preserved in the Tower.
There to be prisoned; where, their blame to quite;
They each other these Epistles write.
Mine one dear Lord, sith thou art locked from me,
In this disguise my love must steal to thee,
Since to Renew all Loves, all Kindness past,
This refuge scarcely left, yet this the last.
My keeper coming, I of thee inquire,
Who with thy greeting answers my desire;
Which my Tongue willing to return again,
Grief stops my words, and I but strive in vain,
Where with amazed, away in haste he goes,
When through my lips my heart thrusts forth my woes,
But then the Doors that make a doleful sound,
Drive back my Words, that in the noise are drowned,
Which somewhat hushed, the Echo doth record,
And twice or thrice reiterates my Word;
When like an adverse Wind in Isis course,

Against the Tide bending his boisterous force;
But when the Flood hath wrought it self about,
He following on, doth head-long thrust it out;
Thus strive my Sighs with Tears ever they begin,
And breaking out, again Sighs drive them in.
A thousand forms present my troubled thought,
Yet prove abortive ever they forth are bought.
The depth of Woe with words we hardly sound,
Sorrow is so insensibly profound.
As Tears do fall and rise, Sighs come and go,
So do these numbers ebbe, so do they flow.
These briny Tears do make my Ink look pale,
My Ink clothes Tears in this sad morning vale,
The letters mourners, weep with my dim Eye,
The paper pale, grieved at my misery.
Yet miserable ourselves why should we deem,
 Sith none are so, but in their own esteem?
Who in distress from resolution flys;
Is rightly said, to yield to miseries.
They which begot us, did beget this sin,
They first begun, what did our grief begin,
We tasted not, 'twas they which did rebel,
(Nor our offense) but in their fall we fell;
They which a Crown would to my Lord have linked,
All hope of Life and Liberty extinct;
A Subject born, a Sovereign to have been,
Hath made me now, nor Subject, nor a Queen.
Ah vile Ambition, how doth thou deceive us,
Which showed us Heaven, and yet in Hell doth leave us?
Seldom untouched doth Innocence escape,
When Error commeth in good Counsels shape,
A lawful title counterchecks proud Might,
The weakest things become strong props to right.
Then my dear Lord, although affliction grieve us,
Yet let our spotless Innocence relieve us.

Death but an acted passion doth appear,
Where truth gives Courage & the Conscience clear,
And let thy comfort thus consist in mine.
That I bear part of whatsoever is thine,
As when we lived untouched with these disgraces,
When as our Kingdom was our dear embraces;
At *Durham* Palace, where sweet *Hymen* sang,
Whose Buildings with our Nuptial Music rang:
When *prothalamions* praised that happy day,
Wherein great *Dudley* matched with noble *Gray*,
When they devised to link by Wedlock's Band,
The House of Suffolk to Northumberland,
Our fatal Dukedom to your Dukedom bound,
To frame this Building on so weak a Ground.
For what avails a lawless usurpation,
Which gives a Scepter, but not rules a Nation?
Only the surest of a vain Opinion:
What gives Content, gives what exceeds Dominion.
When first mine Ears were pierced with the Fame,
Of *Jane*, proclaimed by a Princes Name,
A sudden fright my trembling heart appalls:
The fear of Conscience entreat upon Walls:
Thrice happy for our Fathers had it been,
If What we feared, they wisely had foreseen,
And kept a mean gate, in an humble Path,
To have escaped the Heavens impetuous wrath,
To true bred Eagle strongly stems the wind,
And not each Bird resembling their brave Kind:
He like a King, doth from the clouds command
The fearful Fowl, that move but near the Land.
Though *Mary* be from mighty Kings descended,
My blood not from *Plantagenet* pretended;
My Grandfather *Brandon* did our house advance,
By Princely *Mary* Dowager of *France*;
The Fruit of that fair Stock, which did combine,

And *York*'s sweet Branch with *Lancaster*'s entwine,
And in one Stalk did happily unite
The pure Vermillion Rose, and purer White;
I, the untimely Slip of that rich Stem,
Whose golden Bud brings forth a Diadem.
But oh, forgive me Lord, it is not I,
Nor do I boast of this, but learn to die:
While we were as ourselves, conjoined then,
Nature to Nature, now an Alien.
To gain a Kingdom, who spares their next blood?
Nearness contemned, if Sovereignty withstood.
A Diadem once dazzling the Eye,
The day too dark to see infinity;
And where the Army is stretched to reach a Crown;
Friendship is broke, the dearest things thrown down:
For what great *Henry* most strove to avoid,
The Heavens have built, where Earth would have destroyed
And seating *Edward* on his Regal Throne,
He gives to *Mary* all that was his own,
By death assuring what by Life is theirs,
The Lawful claim of *Henrys* lawful heirs,
By mortal Laws the bond may be divorced,
But Heavens decree by no means can be forced:
That rules the case, when men have all decreed,
Who took him hence foresaw who should succeed,
For we in vain rely on humane Laws,
When in Heaven stands forth to plead the righteous cause,
Thus rule the Skies in their continual course,
That yields to Fate, that doth not yield to force.
Mans wit doth build for Time but to devourer,
But virtue free from Time and Fortunes power.
Then, my kind Lord, sweet *Gilford,* be not grieved,
The soul is Heavenly, and from Heaven relieved:
And as we once have plighted Troth together,
Now let us make exchange of Minds to either;

To thy fair breast take my resolved Mind,
Armed against black despair, and all her kind,
Into my bosom breath that Soul of thine,
There to be made as perfect as is mine;
So shall our faiths as firmly be approved,
As I of thee, or thou of me beloved.
This Life, no Life, wert thou not dear to me,
Nor this no Death, were I not woe for thee.
Thou my dear Husband, and my Lord before,
But truly learn to Die, thou shalt be more.
Now live by Prayer, on Heavenly fix all thy thought,
And surely find, what ever by zeal is sought;
For each good motion that the Soul awakes,
A Heavenly figure sees, from whence it takes
That sweet Remembrance, which by power of kind,
Forms (like it self) an Image in the mind,
And in our Faith the operations be,
Of that Divineness which through that we see;
Which never erres, but accidentally,
By our frail Fleshes imbecility;
By each Temptation over-apt to slide.
Except our Spirit becomes our bodies guide;
For as these Towers our bodies do enclose,
So our Souls prison verily are those:
Our bodies, stopping that Celestial light,
As these do hinder our exterior sight,
Whereon Death seizing, doth discharge the debt,
And us at blessed Liberty doth set.
Then draw thy Forces all up to thy Heart,
The strongest Fortress of this Earthly part,
And on these three let thy assurance lie,
On Faith, Repentance, and Humility;
By which, to Heaven ascending by degrees,
Persist in Prayer upon your bended Knees:
Whereon if you assuredly be stayed,

You need in Peril not to be dismayed,
Which still shall keep you, that you shall not fall,
For any peril that can you appall:
The Key of Heaven thus with you, you shall bear,
And Grace you guiding get you entrance there;
And you of those Celestial Joys possess,
Which mortal Tongues unable to express.
Then thank the Heaven, preparing us this Room,
Crowning our Heads with glorious Martyrdom,
Before the black and dismal days begin,
The days of all Idolatry and sin;
Not suffering us to see that wicked Age,
When Persecution vehemently shall rage;
When tyranny new Tortures shall invent,
To inflict Vengeance on the Innocent.
Yet Heaven forbid, that *Mary's* Womb should bring
England's fair Scepter to a foreign King;
But she to fair *Elizabeth* shall leave it,
Which broken, hurt, and wounded shall receive it:
And on her Temples having placed the Crown,
Root out the dregges Idolatry hath sown;
And *Syons* glory shall again restore,
Laid ruin, waste, and desolate before;
And from black Cinders, and rude heaps of Stones;
Shall gather up the Martyrs scared bones;
And shall extrip the Power of *Rome* again,
And cast aside the heavy Yoke of *Spain.*
Farewell, sweet *Guilford,* know our End is near,
Heaven is our Home, we are but strangers here:
Let us make haste to go unto the blest,
Which from these weary Worldly Labors rest.
And with these Lines, my dearest Lord, I greet thee,
Until in Heaven thy *Jane* again shall meet thee.

Annotations of the Chronicle History.

They which begot us, did beget this sin.
Showing the ambition of the two Dukes, their Fathers, whose pride was the cause of the utter overthrow of their children.

At *Durham* Palace, where sweet *Hymen* sang.
The Buildings, &c.

The Lord Guilford Dudley, forth son to *John Dudley*, Duke of *Northumberland*, married the Lady Jane *Gray* daughter to the Duke of *Suffolk*, at *Durham* House in the *Strand.*

When first mine Ears were pierced with fame of Jane, proclaimed by Princess Name.

Presently upon the death of King *Edward,* the Lady *Jane* was taken as Queen, conveyed by Water to the *Tower* of *London,* for her safety and after proclaimed in divers parts of the Realm, as so ordained by King *Edwards* letters patents, and his will.

My Grandfather *Brandon* did our house advance,
By Princely *Mary* Dowager of *France.*

Henry Gray, *Duke of* Suffolk, *married* Frances, *the eldest daughter of* Charles Brandon, *Duke of* Suffolk, *by the* French *Queen; by which* Frances, *he had this Lady* Jane: *This* Mary, *the* French *Queen, was daughter to King* Henry *the Seventh, by* Elizabeth *his Queen; which happy marriage conjoined the two Noble Families* Lancaster *and* York.

For what great Henry most strove to avoid.

Noting the distrust that King Henry the eight ever had in the Princes Mary, his daughter, fearing she should alter the fate of

Religion in the Land, by matching with a Stranger, confessing the Right that King Henries issue had to the Crown.

But unto faire Elizabeth shall leave it.

A Prophesy of Queen Mary's Barrenness, and of the happy and glorious Reign of Queen Elizabeth; her restoring of Religion, the abolishing of the Romish Servitude, and casting aside the Yoke of Spain.

SECOND POEM

Gilford Dudley to the Lady Jane Gray.

As the Swan singing at his dying Hour,
So I reply from my imprisoning Tower;
O, could there be that power but in my Verse,
T' express the Grief which my sad Heart doth pierce!
The very Walls that straightly thee enclose,
Would surely weep at reading of my woes;
Let your Eyes lend, I'll pay you every Tear,
And give you interest, you if doe forbear,
Drop for a Drop, and if you'll needs have Lone,
I will repay you frankly, two for one.
Perhaps you'll think (your sorrows to appease)
That words of comfort fitter were then these.
True, and in you when such perfection liveth,
As in most grief, me now most comfort giveth,
But think not *Jane* that cowardly I faint,
To beg mans mercy by my sad complaint,
That Death so much my courage can control,
At the departing of my living soul.
For if one life a thousand lives could be,
All those too few to consummate with thee,

When thou this Cross so patiently does bear,
As if thou were incapable of fear,
And does no more this dissolution fly,
Then if long Age constrained thee to die.
Yet it is strange thou art become my Foe,
And only now adds most unto my woe;
Not that I loath what most did me delight,
But that so long deprived of thy sight:
For when I speak and would complain my wrong,
Straight-ways thy Name possess all my Tong,
As thou before me evermore did lie,
The present Object to my longing eye.
No ominous Star did at thy Birth-tide shine,
That might of thy sad destine divine;
'Tis only I that did thy fall persuade,
And thou by me a Sacrifice art made,
As in those Countries, where the loving Wives,
With their kind Husbands end their happy Lives,
And crowned with Garlands, in their Brides attire,
Burn with his Body, in the Funeral fire;
And she the worthiness reckoned is of all,
Whom least the Peril seem to appall.
I boast not of *Northumberland's* great Name,
(Nor of *Kent* conquered, adding to our Fame)
When he to *Norfolk* with his Armies sped,
And then in Chaynes the Rebels capture led,
And brought safe Peace returning to our Doors,
Yet spread his Glory on the Eastern Shores;
Nor of my Brothers, from whose natural Grace,
Virtue may spring, to beautify our Race;
Nor of *Grays* Match, my Children born by thee,
Of the great Blood undoubtedly to be:
But of thy Virtue only do I boast,
That wherein I, may justly glory most.
I craved no Kingdoms, though I thee did crave,

It me sufficed, thy only self to have:
Yet let me say, however it befell,
Me thinks a Crown should have becomed thee well;
For sure thy Wisedom merited (or none)
To have been heard with Wonder from a Throne.
When from thy Lips the counsel to each deed,
Doth as from some wise Oracle proceed;
And more esteemed thy Virtues were to me,
Then all that else might ever come by thee:
So chaste thy Love, so innocent thy Life,
As being a Virgin when thou were a wife;
So great a Gift the Heaven on me bestowed,
As giving that, it nothing could have owned,
Such was the Good I did Possess of late,
Were Worldly Care disturbed our quiet state;
Were Trouble did in every place abound,
And angry War our former Peace did wound.
But to know this, Ambition us affords,
One Crown is guarded with a thousand Swords;
To mean estates, mean Sorrows are but shown,
But crowns have cares, whose workings be unknown.
When *Dudley* led his Armies to the East,
Of our whole Forces generally possest,
What then was thought his Enterprise could let,
Whom a grave Counsel freely did abet,
That had the Judgment of the powerful Laws,
In every Point to justify the Cause?
The holy Church a helping hand that laid, (swade?)
Who would have thought that these could not have,
But what alas can Parliament avail,
Where *Mary's* right must *Edward's* acts repeal?
When *Suffolk's* power doth *Suffolk's* hopes withstand,
Northumberland doth leave Northumberland;
And they that should our Greatness undergo,
Us, and our actions only overthrow.

Were greatness gained, we give it all our heart,
But being once come, we with it would depart,
And indescretly follow that so fast,
Which overtaken punish our haste,
If any one do pity our offense,
Let him be sure that he be far from hence:
Here is no place for any one that shall,
So much as (once) commensurate our fall,
And we of mercy vainly should but think,
Our timeless Tears then insatiate earth doth drink.
All lamentations utterly forlorn,
Dying before they fully can be born.
Mothers that should their woeful Children rue,
Fathers in death to kindly bid adue,
Friends their dear farewell lovingly to take,
The faithful Servant weeping for our sake;
Brothers and Sisters waiting on our Beer,
Mourners to tell what we were living here,
But we (alas) deprived are of all,
So fatal is our miserable fall.
And where at first for safety we were shut,
Now in dark Prison woefully are put,
And from the height of our ambitious state,
Lie to repent our arrogance too late.
To thy persuasion thus I then reply,
Hold on thy course resolved still to die,
And when we shall so happily be gone,
Leave it to heaven to give the rightful Throne,
And with that health regret I thee again,
Which I of late did gladly entertain.

Annotations of the Chronicle Historic.

Nor of Kent conquered, adding to our fame.

John, Duke of *Northumberland*, when before he was Earl of *Warwick*, in his Expedition against *Kent*, overthrew the Rebels of *Norfolk* and *Suffolk*, encamped at *Mount-Surrey* in *Norfolk*.

Nor of my Brothers, from whose natural grace.

Guilford Dudley, is remembering in this place the towardness of his brothers, which were all likely indeed to have raised that house of the Dudley's, of which he was a forth Brother, if not Suppressed by their Father's Overthrow.

Nor of Grays Match, my Children born by thee.

Noting in this place the Alliance of the Lady *Jane Gray* by her Mother, which was *Frances*, the daughter of *Charles Brandon*, by *Mary* the *French* Queen, daughter to *Henry* the seventh, and sister to *Henry* the eighth.

To have been heard with wonder from a Throne.

Seldom has it ever been known of any Woman enluded [*sic*] with such wonderful gifts, as was this Lady both for her Wisdom and Learning: Of whose skill in the tongues, one reported by this Epigram;

Mitaris Inanam Graio sermone valere?
Quo primum nata est tempore Graia fuit.

When Dudley led his Army to the East.

The Duke of *Northumberland* prepared his Power at *London*; for his expedition against the Rebels in *Norfork* and making hast away appointed the rest of his Forces to meet him at *New-Market Heath*: of whom, this saying is reported, that passing through *Shore-Ditch*, the Lord *Gray* in his company, seeing the People in great numbers came to see him, he said; The people press to see us, but none bid God speed us.

Whom a grave counsel freely did abet.

John Dudley, Duke of *Northumberland*, when he went out against Queen *Mary* had his commission sealed for the Generalship of the Army, by the consent of the whole counsel of the land: insomuch, that passing through the counsel chamber at his departure, the Earl of *Arundel* wished, That he might have gone with him in that expedition, and to spend his Blood in the quarrel.

When Suffolk's *Power doth* Suffolk's *Hopes withstand*, Northumberland *doth leave* Northumberland.

The *Suffolk* men were that first that ever resorted to Queen *Mary* in her distress, repairing to her successors, while she remained both at *Kenninghall*, and *Fremingham* castle, still increasing her Aids, until the Duke of *Northumberland* was left forsaken at *Cambridge* [Drayton 335].

The last item is an epistle said to be from Lady Jane to Guildford. Though very different from the poem that Jane wrote to Guildford in the Drayton edition, some passages read as though they were composed by Jane. The title page claims it was "Supposed to have been written in the Tower, a few Days before they suffered." That is not conclusive proof of its authorship, but it merits included in this volume, as well as the advertisement by the original editor which precedes the poem.

The book *An Epistle from Lady Jane Grey to Lord Guildford Dudley* was dedicated to The Right Honorable Mary Lepel, Baroness Dowager Hervey of Ickworth and published by George Keate, London, in 1762.

Advertisement.

Lady Jane Grey hath ever been regarded, as one of the most amiable and perfect Characters, that the Records of any Nation have delivered down to Posterity. The Circumstances of her Life are uncommon, if not unexampled, and her Misfortunes as singular, as was the Fortitude with which she sustained them; all conspiring to render her a fit Subject for this Species of Heroic Poetry, of which we have but few Pieces in our Language; tho' it seems to have a peculiar Advantage of conveying, in the happiest Manner, the Sentiments of such Characters as are worthy of being cele-brated.

The Variety of Accomplishments, which this unfortunate Prin-cess crowded into the short Period of seventeen Years, and above all, that Justness of thinking which she attained in so early an Age, have deservedly gained her the Admiration of succeeding times.

But her Story is so well known, that it would be Impertinence to dwell upon it. Wedded to a Man she loved, and whose Youth and Virtues made him worthy of her Affection, called to a Crown against her Will, throned and dethroned within the little Com-pass of a Fortnight, dragged from her palace to her Prison, sepa-rated from a Husband doomed to death, and sentenced to lose her own Head on the Scaffold; Such were the Distresses that sur-rounded her, when I ventured to put the Pen into her Hand: awake as she was, to every Passion and Delicacy of Sentiment, which Love, Disappointment, and Calamity could give Birth to; yet, by the Force of Religion, subduing their Poignancy, and at last totally triumphing over them.

I much doubt whether I may have done sufficient Justice to the Character of this virtuous Lady; but hope at least, that I have not departed from Nature, in any Sentiment which I have attributed to her.

Lady Jane Gray to Lord Guildford Dudley.

From these dread Walls, this melancholy Tower,
Doomed the sad victim of relentless Power,
Where Ruin sits in gloomy pomp arrayed,
And circling Horrors spread their mournful shade,
I send the Tribute of a shortening Life,5
The last Memorial of a faithful Wife.
For every Hope on this Side Heaven is fled,
And Death's pale Banner waves around my head.
It yet perchance may cheer my Lord to know
That Suffolk's Daughter sinks not with her Woe:10
Beneath it's weight I feel myself resigned;
Tho' strong the Tempest, stronger still my mind.
This Duty paid to thee, each Care is over,
Nor my hard Fortune shall distress me more.

Yet spite of all, one anxious Thought survives,15
For thee, my Guildford, 'tis for thee it lives.
Yes, thou alone with Heaven divided my Heart,
Tho' all Heaven's Due, yet Nature gives thee Part.
If Love be still a Crime, I'm guilty still,
But to forget depends not on our Will.20
Affection once deep rooted in the breast,
Is sometimes shook, tho' rarely dispossest;
The ruling Passion there in Triumph reigns,
It sooths my Weakness, but augments my Pains.
Over the dear past my roving Fancy Flies,25
And brings thy image to my raptured Eyes,
No Mourner's Weeds, no Captive's Chain it wears,
But bright in all its native Charms appears;
Such Grace, such Virtue beaming from thy Brows,
As stole my Heart, and fixed my virgin Vows,30
At Hymen's Alter such thy Form was seen
When late we offered to the Cyprian Queen.
How little thought we while the flowery Wreath
Intwinded our Temples, it was wove by Death!
Far different Scenes the Syren Hope displayed;35
Ah! How the False One sung, and how betrayed!
Each joy she promised perished in it's birth,
And every flattering Blossom fell to Earth!
But from Man's Weakness still some Comfort flows,
'Tis that he nought beyond the present knows;40
Heaven draws a friendly Curtin over his Doom,
And hides in deepest Shades each ill to come.
Then be it's Will adored, which, understood,
From seeming Mischief draws forth certain Good.
Nor in these Lines suspect that I complain,45
Tho' Memory loves to tread back Time again.

Thus do I waste the solitary Day,
With tedious Pace thus creep my Hours away;
And if, when Cynthia, robbed in paler Light,
Revisits Mortals, and directs the Night,50
My wearied Strength the general Slumber shares,
The Soul reflecting wakes to all her Cares:
Delusion over my Mind usurps Command,
And rules each Sense with Fancy's magic Wand.

One Moment Tidings of Forgiveness brings,55
Descending Mercy spreads her Cherub Wings;
Our Guards had vanished, every Grief effaced,
We meet again, embracing and embraced.
O' Bliss supreme! — but too supreme to last;
Ere Words can find their Way, the Vision's past:60
It fleets, I call it back, — it will not hear,
And fearful Shadows in it's Place appear.
The unrelenting Queen stalks fiercely by,
Fate on her Brow, and Fury in her Eye.
Hark! The dread Signal that completes our Woes!65
Hark! The loud Shoutings of our barbarous Foes!
I see the Axe reared high above thy Head,
It falls! — and Guildford's numbered with the Dead.
Alas! how ghastly! every Vein streams Blood,
And the pale Corps sinks in the crimson Flood.70
Could that sad Form be once my Soul's Delight?
Quick tear the maddening Phantom from my Sight.
Hold, hold your Hands, ye Ministers of Fate,
Suspend the Blow, lest Mercy come too late;
Let Innocence at last your Pity move,75
And spare my lord, my Husband, and my Love!
Northumberland! thee, thee could I upbraid,
And bid thee view the Ruin thou hast made.
This mournful Picture thy Ambition planned,
And all it's Colors own thy daring Hand.80
But thou art fallen! — nor shall my parting Breath
Call out for Vengeance in the Hour of Death:
All now is over, the fatal Woof is spun,
The destined Labor of the Sisters done.
May all Remembrance of the Guilt subside,85
And the dark Grave thy Dust and Frailties hide.

The searching Eye of Heaven, whose Wisdom darts
Through all the mean Disguises of our Hearts,
And every silent Motive, knows alone
With what Reluctance I approached the Throne.90
I never sighed for Grandeur's envied Rays,
For regal Honors, or a Nations Praise.
My Bosom never felt Ambition's Fire;
For what Exchange could Guildford's Wife desire?
The Bloom of May beneath our Feet was spread,95

And all it's Roses decked our nuptial Bed.
With thee conjoined, each social Joy I found;
With thee conversing, Pleasure breathed around.
To prize the World aright, and from the Mind
To my loved Books my Leisure I resigned:100
Or absent thou, to cheer the Evening's Gloom,
Encircled with my Maidens, plyed the Loom.
Peace was my Sister, and my Friend Content,
The best Companions ever to Mortals sent;
Placed at my Side they turned their soothing Lyres,105
And sung those Carols Innocence inspires.
But when, obedient to a Father's Power,
And the last Wish of Edward's dying hour,
Destructive Counsel! I my Home forsook,
Assumed the Purple, and the Scepter took,110
Swift from my Sight the heavenly Pair withdrew,
And Friend and Sister bade me both adieu.

Let such as, flattered by a pompous Name,
Risk their own Quiet in Pursuit of Fame,
Beware the Exchange; awhile their Purpose turn,115
And from a wretched Queen one Moral learn.
It is the Cheat of every worldly joy
To tempt when distant, but possessed to cloy.
Hence flows a Truth of much Import, 'tis this;
"Content's the highest Pitch of human Bliss."120
Strange we should then the proffered Boon reject!
All know to seek it, yet the Search neglect.
To no one soil, no Station 'tis confined,
Springing, if cultured, in each steady Mind,
Far from Ambition's fiery Tract it flies,125
But lives with Virtue, and with Virtue dies!

O had our Lot by kinder Stars been thrown
Beneath some lonely Shade to Fame unknown;
Far from those Scenes removed where Pride resorts,
Far from the Cares, far from the Crimes of Courts.130
Unconscious of the Thorns which wound the Great,
Our lengthened Years had owned a happier Fate:
Pleasured with our Fortune, by ourselves approved,
Secure from Envy, and by all beloved.
While, from a busy, faithless World retired,135

By no blind Folly vexed, no passion fired,
Calmly we then afar had heard the Strife,
The Noise, the Tumult that perplexes Life;
Smiled at Contention's visionary Plan,
And the vain Toils of self-deluded Man.140

Yet cease, my Heart, these plaintive Murmurs cease;
For why, my Guildford, should I wound thy Peace?
Why with Elysian Dreams thy Thoughts engage,
While we are fettered on a tragic Stage?
But say, what Tyranny can reach the Soul?145
What Terrors shake her, or what Force control?
Immortal as the Power from whence she springs,
Sick of her Home, she mounts on Fancy's Wings,
With inborn Freedom nourished, spurns her Chains,
And roves unbounded through ideal Scenes!150
Ideal Joys are all I now have left,
Of thee, a Crown, and Liberty bereft;
Torn from the Pleasures of domestic life,
From each fond Rapture of a virtuous Wife:
By all Hope here forsaken! 'tis in vain155
That Reason whispers I should not complain:
A Sigh will heave, in Spite of all my powers;
And Sighs are due to Miseries like Ours.
Ha! Meet no more! — how cruel the Decree! —
Heart-rendering Sentence! — no — it must not be.160
Down Prison Walls, each Obstacle remove,
And let me clasp once more the Man I love.
One parting Look a wretched Wife desires;
One parting Kiss the Seal of Death requires! —
And is there none to plead the unhappy Suit? —165
All Ears are deaf, and every Tongue is mute! —
Then, come the worst — Yet, howsoever distrest,
Still shall thy Image live within my Breast;
My senses still that Object shall pursue,
And each fond Wish be offered up for you.170
Tho' all unfeeling for this bleeding Heart,
Our Foes dismiss to Heaven thy nobler Part,
Deep in the Dust thy injuried Form I'll trace,
And grudge the unconscious Grave it's cold Embrace.
But hold thy hand, presumptuous Woman, hold;175
Too warm thy Passion, as thy Pen to bold.

Far other Thoughts the present Hour demands,
Lo! at my Side the shadowy Monarch stands;
Aid me, great Teacher, this hard Conflict end,
Tho' King of Terrors called, I'll hail thee Friend!180
Since thou alone portrayed to Mortal Eyes
How weak, how baseless are the Joys we prize:
Thou mock our useless Toils, our mimic State,
And warn a Brother, by a Brother's Fate!
Thy Moral then shall not be lost on me,185
Convinced, my Soul approves the just Decree;
And unrepining quits this Scene of Strife,
Which points through Virtue to a happier Life.

The Priest this Morn, with every Art Endued,
The accursed Purpose hath again renewed;190
"Be ours," he cries, "our better Faith embrace,
"And live Preserver of your falling Race.
"Tho' yet misled, stand forth the Child of Rome,
"The Queen in Mercy will avert your Doom."
Merciful Queen! — yet since thus greatly kind195
Tell us what Mercy shall the Apostate find?
Thy royal Mandate may decide our Fates,
But Peace alone on conscious Duty waits.
Who wars against it, does the Work of Hell,
And arms a Demon he can never quell;200
Whose Shafts received, search the wide Globe around,
Nor Herb, nor balsam heals the fatal Wound.
Bear back, false Winchester, thy proffered Bliss,
Weigh Crowns and Kingdoms with a Deed like this,
Far, far too light in Wisdom's Eye they seem,205
Nor shake and Scale, while Reason holds the Beam.
And can she, Guildford, deem me sunk so low,
So fondly wedded to this World of Woe,
To think her Bounty would my Fears entice
To purchase fleeting Breath at such a Price?210
Which when obtained, the poor precarious Toy
A Thousand Ills might weaken or destroy?
No — since I'm sworn a Sister to mischance,
Let the Clouds gather, let the Storm advance,
Unmoved, it's bursting Horrors I'll defy,215
And steady to my Faith a Martyr die.
For Life's alas! too like the transient Rose,

Which oft is blasted the same Day it blows;
It's Beauty from the Wind a Blight receives,
Or some foul Canker taints it's crimson Leaves!220
Nor judge it hard to fall an early Flower,
Rescued perchance from some tempestuous Shower,
From noxious Vapors armed with a Force to kill,
The Noontide Sunbeam, or the Evening Chill.
However the Thought appal, Death's gloomy Road225
By every mortal Foot must once be trod!
Deep through the Vale of Tears Man's Journey lies,
And Sorrow best prepares him for the Skies!
O then my Husband, I conjure thee, hear,
If Suffolk's Daughter ever to thee was dear,230
By every Wish of Happiness to come,
By every Hope beyond the mouldring Tomb;
If anxious that thy better Fame should soar,
And shine applauded when the Man's no more:
Let not the wily Churchman win thine Ear,235
Or sooth thy Weakness by his fraudful Care;
But armed with Constancy's unfailing Shield,
As God's own Soldier valiant, scorn to yield.
So when Religion stripped of each Disguise,
In ancient Purity again shall rise,240
To her true Throne once more shall be restored,
And rule by Reason, stronger than the Sword,
Posterity our Merits may attest,
And our fair Deeds by all good Men be blest.
In distant Times then shall old People tell,245
How firmly Guildford and his Consort fell.
To all their listing Family relate,
How our Faith triumphed, tho' our Woes were great.
Then shall each Youth and Maid our Names revere,
Grace our sad Story with a generous Tear,250
And give our Dust this Requiem with a Sigh,
"Peace guard the Shrine where Virtue's Children Lie!

O Thou Supreme, on whom we all depend,
Our common Parent, and our common Friend,
Who deignest to watch us from thy distant Skies,255
Bidding the Prayers of humbled Sufferers rise,
Ruler of heaven, stretch forth thy mighty Hand,
And save from civil Rage my native Land.

175

Let Rome's ambitious Sons no more prevail,
Blast all their Hopes, and let their Counsels fail.260
Raise up some Prince to perfect that great Plan
Thy Servant Edward (under Thee) began;
That Error's Clouds dispersed may never return,
And thy pure Light with Fires rekindled burn.
So Peace, sad Fugitive, again shall smile,265
And fix her Dwelling on this prospered Isle.
While for myself one only Boon I crave,
Support that Fortitude thy Mercy gave;
The Heart thou madest preserve severely just,
Firm in it's Fate, and steady to its Trust.270
There, while it beats, thy Praise shall ever reign,
Live, while it lives, and flow in every Vein:
Praise the sole Tribute I have left to give,
Nay, all a God from Mortals can receive.

Come then, my Lord, my Husband, and my Love,275
(For death alone those Titles shall remove)
With decent Courage meet thy certain Doom,
Nor shrink with Horror at the opening Tomb.
What's in the Grave the virtuous have to fear?
'Tis Peace, 'tis Refuge from the worst Despair:280
All Strife, all human Contests 'twill adjust,
Nor can the Hand of Power insult the Dust!
Religion sitting by the Mourner's Side
Inspires that Comfort which the World denied;
And, amidst our Woes, of this one Truth we're sure,285
Whatever is mortal cannot long endure.
Our Pains, as well as Joys, soon find an End,
And, tired of both, we call our Shroud a Friend!
Meet it such, my Guildford, nor thy Soul
Overawe with Fancy, or with Fear control.290
Think, 'twill the Rigor of thy Lot repay,
Think, 'tis a Passport to the Realms of Day.
On Faith's strong Pinions thou shalt wing thy Flight,
And (the World conquered) with the Blest unite.
The Pomp of Death, the Scaffold, and the Steel,295
The Man recoiling may an Instant feel,
For the Nature will be heard; but be thy Mind.
Warm with it's future Prospects, and resigned.
What then remains for me? — Ah! Wherefore ask?

Fain would my trembling Pen avoid the Task;300
Here would it stop, nor wake thy sufferings more,
But idle Ceremony now is over;
These Tear-stained Lines must their whole purpose tell,
And bid my dying Lord a last Farewell.
A last! A long Farewell! — Oh cruel Sound!305
It pains, it tears, it harrows up my Wound.
Alas! the transient Dream! — Down, Rebel Heart,
Yet, keen their Pangs that must for ever part!
A Thousand, Thousand Things I had to say,
But the fleet Minutes suffer no Delay.310
Might these fond Eyes once more that Form behold,
These Arms, 'tho 'twere in Death, my Love enfold!
A Woman's Weakness sure might be forgiven,
And this last Frailty be absolved by Heaven.
'Twas a rash Wish; — no — shun me, — for I fear315
A final Interview we could not bear!
Ere yet a little Space, this Scene will close,
And end the Malice of our ruthless Foes.
Armed as we are for Fate, we'll die content;
Fortune hath done it's worst, it's Rage is spent.320
To happier mansions we shall soon remove,
And meet in Bliss, for we shall meet above.
Crowned with eternal Peace, we then shall own
How poor the Contest for a worldly Throne!
No Feuds, no Treasons can our Joys molest,325
Or shake the immortal Triumphs of the Blest.
And see, our wished-for Haven is not far,
This Hope shall cheer us like a guiding Star;
Safe in our Sea-beat Bark we'll stem the Flood,
And spread each Sail to meet the coming Good.330
Descend, my Guardian Angel, from the Skies,
In my firm Breast let dauntless Virtue rise;
Loose, loose all Ties that hold me captive here,
And from my memory blot what most was dear.
Yes, my Deliverer, yes, I find thy Aid;335
Each Passion's calm, and all the Storm is laid.
I felt its Influence, Guildford, as I spoke,
The complicated Chain at length is broke.
Life's vain Enchantments all have taken their Flight,
And Earth diminished fades before my sight.340
One last, sad, parting Sigh is left for you;

The rest is heaven's: — a long — long — long Adieu!

Finis [Keate 1].

No less speculative than the other material in this chapter are the inscriptions in the Tower of London attributed to Lady Jane. These exist in many variations; those from *The History and Antiquities of the Tower of London* by John Bayley, and the *Literary Remains of Lady Jane Grey* by Nicholas Harris Nicolas, Esq., have been selected, here, because of those authors' historical accuracy and thoroughness.

Beside a small window in the staircase, the name of Edmund Poole is inscribed twice. Immediately beneath the inscription of Edmund Poole is the word IANE, generally accepted to be from the hand of Lady Jane. Sir John reports that her name once also appeared on another side of the room but was destroyed when a window was added.

A likely conjecture is that the two inscriptions, instead of being made by Lady Jane herself, were cut by Guildford, just as a lover would carve his beloved's name into a tree.

When a woman of distinction was committed to the Tower, she was usually confined in the private house of the lieutenant or some other respectable officer of the fortress. It is highly unlikely that Jane and Guildford would have been placed together.

In addition to the name IANE inscribed in the Tower, the following incisions, cut into the walls with a pin, have also been attributed to Lady Jane, though here again there is no conclusive proof that the words were actually written by Jane Grey.

Non aliena putes homini quae obtingere possunt,
Sors hodierna mihi, cras erit illa tibi!

To mortals' common fate thy mind resign,
My lot to day, to-morrow may be thine.

Sir Nicholas includes in *Literary Remains of Lady Jane Grey* the following verse, which was also incised with a pin.

Deo juvante, nil nocet livor malus;
Et non juvante, nil juvat labor gravis:
Post tenebras, spero lucem.

Whilst God assists us, envy bites in vain,
If God forsake us, fruitless all our pain —
I hope for light after the darkness [Nicholas 61].

In researching this work, the author also discovered a play about Lady Jane, *The Tragedy of the Lady Jane Gray as it is acted at the Theatre-Royal in Drury-Lane,* by N. Rowe, Esquire. It was printed in London for Bernard Lintott at the Cross-Keys between the Temple-Gates in Fleetstreet in 1715.

CHAPTER 5. CROSS-EXAMINATION

A research project that sets out to answer specific questions inevitably raises more questions when those have been answered. The reillumination of the "Lane Letters" after nearly 200 years has clarified many issues, but certainly has raised many more.

One of the most compelling unanswered questions deals with Mary Grey, Lady Jane's younger sister. Among the multitude of documents presented in this edition, how many letters or records mention Mary Grey? Other than the Grey family tree, none. Mary Grey did, in fact, exist. References to her often mention her husband, Thomas Keyes. Three such references are included here. The first is from the 1675 edition of the *Annals of England*, in which Mr. Godwin reports, "the Duke of Suffolk's youngest daughters are married, Catherine to Lord Henry eldest son to the Earl of Pembroke, and crouch-backed Mary to Martin Keyes Groom Porter" (Godwin, 148).

The second is from the 1691 edition of *The History of the Reformation*. Burnet writes,

> about the end of May or beginning of June, the Duke of Suf-
> folk's three daughters were married: the eldest. Lady Jane, to the

Lord Guildford Dudley, the forth son to the Duke of Northumberland. The Second, the Lady Katherine, to the Earl of Pembroke's eldest son, the Lord Herbert. The third, the Lady Mary, who was crooked, to the Kings Groom Porter Martin Keyes" [Burnet, Part 2, 222].

The last reference is from the 1677 edition of *A Genealogical History of the Kings of England and Monarchs of Great Britain*, by Francis Sanford.

> And now were the three daughters of Henry Grey Duke of Suffolk (which he had by Frances daughter of Charles Brandon and Mary Queen of France) married at Durham House; Jane the eldest, to the Lord Guildford Dudley fourth son to the Duke of Northumberland; Katherine, the second, to Henry eldest Son and Heir of William Herbert Earl of Pembroke, and Mary, the youngest, (being somewhat deformed) to Henry Keyes the Kings Gentleman Porter [Sanford, Appendix].

History records no events of Mary's life other than that in early 1564, when she was about nineteen, she became involved with Thomas Keyes. This bit of information places her birth at about 1545, some eight years after Lady Jane.

A few references describe her as a "Dwarf Princess," indicating that she was short and slightly deformed by a hump in her back. Her disposition has been said to be a combination of Jane's and Catherine's.

In the summer of 1565, Mary married Thomas Keyes, Queen Elizabeth's Sergeant-Porter, a middle-aged widower with several children. The circumstances surrounding the marriage were controversial, and the Star Chamber declared their marriage a "pretended wedlock." Mary was sent away from court to live with a couple in Buckinghamshire, and Thomas Keyes was imprisoned in the fleet where he remained until his death in 1571.

Oddly, Jane did not mention her younger sister in any letter. Lady Jane wrote and received letters from her sister Catherine and mentions her several times in other letters. Is it possible that Mary's deformity embarrassed the family? Or that letters written to or received from her have either been lost or remain buried in some obscure book or in a collection of manuscripts somewhere in the world? I would like to believe the latter.

An equally compelling subject is the source of the "Lane Letters." *Lady Jane Grey, an Historical Tale in 2 volumes*, was printed for William Lane in London at the Minerva Press in 1791. No clue is given anywhere else in the book's 191 pages. The last page is an advertisement for the "The Novelist, a monthly publication embellished with beautiful engravings with a selection of Tales, Histories, Adventures and Anecdotes from the best modern publications. Printed for William Lane at the Minerva Press."

A review of three of the five known copies, one in the British Library, one in the William Andrews Clark Memorial Library at the University of California Los Angeles, and the third in the Alderman Memorial Library at the University of Virginia, has yielded no new information about the origin or source of the letters. The editions appear to be identical to each other.

Fortunately, there are records of the Minerva Press. A remarkable book dealing only with the history of the press was published in 1939: *The Minerva Press 1790-1820*, by Dorothy Blakey. This very comprehensive study reports that a copy of *Lady Jane Grey, an Historical Tale* had been examined and that "no conjecture as to the authorship can be offered."

Probably, while William Lane worked at the Minerva Press, he purchased the original manuscript from an anonymous contributor. This is suggested by the following note from *The Star*, June 26, 1792: "This may well be called the age of Novels, when Lane, at the Minerva, Leadenhall-Street, has paid near Two Thousand Pounds for Manuscripts" (Blakey 74).

That by no means is conclusive evidence, but it at least shows that Lane was a noted buyer. No evidence suggests the letters are false. Based upon well-documented events, the letters can be used to corroborate other evidence, so they are included in this edition.

A final compelling question is the fate of Lady Jane's and Guildford's bodies after execution. Though there are numerous, often conflicting, descriptions of the execution, there appears to be no record of where the victims' remains were buried. Only two older accounts (pre-1900) mention the location of the graves, and they do not reveal the source of their information.

Some reports indicate burial in the Chapel of St. Peter "ad Vincula," so called from having been consecrated on that festival of the Latin Church, August 1, during the reign of Henry I. The space before the Chapel is called the Tower Green and was used as a burial ground. In the center is a square plot, paved with granite, showing the site where stood the scaffold on which private executions took place. The following persons are known to have been executed on that spot:

1. Lord Hastings, by order of the Duke of Gloucester, in 1483.

2. Queen Anne Boleyn, second wife of Henry VIII, on May 19, 1536.

3. Margaret Countess of Salisbury, the last of the old Angevin or Plantagenet family, on May 27, 1541.

4. Queen Katherine Howard, fifth wife of Henry VIII, on February 13, 1542.

5. Jane Viscountess Rochford on February 13, 1542.

6. Lady Jane Grey, wife of Lord Guildford Dudley, on February 12, 1554.

7. Robert Devereux, Earl of Essex, on February 25, 1601.

All were beheaded with an axe except Queen Anne Boleyn, whose head was struck off with a sword by the executioner of St. Omer, brought over from France for that purpose (Loftie 33).

In 1876, the first resident Governor of the Tower, Colonel Sir Bryan Millman, oversaw the restoration of the Chapel. The stone flooring had to be taken up and replaced, and beneath the stones the bones of hundreds of people; perhaps 1500 bodies, were found. It has been suggested that when the old parish church was moved to its present site, the new location was the old graveyard.

It is a great pity that there is more information about the location of the Duke of Northumberland's body than about those of his own son and daughter-in-law. Perhaps the information currently waits in a manuscript collection, yet unread.

BIBLIOGRAPHY

PRIMARY SOURCES

—. A Catalogue of Additional Manuscripts in the British Museum. London.

Bartlett, David. *The Life of Lady Jane Grey.* Philadelphia: Porter and Coates, 1886.

Beer, Barrett L. *Northumberland: The Political Career of John Dudley.* Kent, Ohio: The Kent State University Press, 1973.

Blakey, Dorothy. *The Minerva Press 1790-1820.* Oxford: Oxford University Press, 1939.

Brown, D. *The History of the Life, Bloody Reign and Death of Queen Mary, Eldest Daughter to Henry VIII.* London, 1682.

Burnet, Gilbert. *The History of the Reformation of the Church of England in Two Parts.* London: J.D. for Richard Chiswell, 1691, 1683 and 1715 editions.

Chapman, Hester W. *Lady Jane Grey — The Nine Day Queen.* London: Jonathan Cape, thirty Bedford Square, 1962.

—. *The Last Tudor King. A Study of Edward VI.* London: Jonathan Cape, thirty Bedford Square, 1958.

—. *Two Tudor Portraits: Henry Howard, Earl of Surry and Lady Katherine Grey.* London: Jonathan Cape, 1960.

Cottonian. A Catalogue of the Manuscripts in the Cottonian Library, Deposited in the British Museum. London: 1802 edition.

187

Dodsley, R. and J. An Epistle from the Lady Jane Gray to Lord Guildford Dudley. Pall-mall, London, 1762.

Ellis, Henry. *Original Letters relative to the English Reformation.* 3 series. London R. Bentley, 1825, 1827 and 1846.

Facciotti, Guglielmo. *L'Historia Ecclesiastica della Rivolvzion.* Printed in Rome, 1594.

Godwin, Francis. *Annals of England: Containing the Reigns of Henry the Eighth, Edward the Sixth, Queen Mary.* London: by W.G. for T. Basset, 1675.

Harding, Rev. Thomas. *The Decades of Henry Bullinger, Minister of the Church of Zurich.* A.M. New York: Johnson Reprint Corp., 1968.

Harley, Robert, Earl of Oxford. Catalogue of the Harleian Collection of Manuscripts in the British Museum. London: D. Leach, 1759 edition.

Heylyn, Peter. Ecclesia Restaurata, or The History of the Reformation of the Church of England. An Appendex to the former book touching the Interposings made in Behalf of the Lady Jane Gray. London: H. Twyford, 1661.

Hoare, Sir Richard Colt. *The History of Modern Wiltshire.* London: by and for J. Nichols and Son, 1843.

Hume, David, Esq. *The History of England.* 6 volumes. London: A. Miller, 1762.

Jordan, Wilbur Kitchener. *Edward VI: The Threshold of Power.* Cambridge: Belknap Press of Harvard University Press, 1970.

Jordan, Wilbur Kitchener. *Edward V:I The Young King.* Cambridge: Belknap Press of Harvard University Press, 1968.

Kempe, Alfred John, Esq. *The Loseley Manuscripts.* London: J. Murry, 1836.

Lane, William. *Lady Jane Grey: An Historical Tale in 2 volumes.* London: The Minerva Press, 1791.

Lansdowne. A Catalogue of the Lansdowne Manuscripts in the British Museum. London England, 1819 edition.

Lindsay, Philip. *The Queenmaker: A Portrait of John Dudley.* London: Williams and Norgate LTD., 1951.

Loach, Jennifer. *Edward VI.* New Haven Connecticut: Yale University Press, 1999.

Loades, David. *John Dudley: Duke of Northumberland 1504-1553.* Oxford: Clarendon Press, 1996.

Loades, David. *Two Tudor Conspiracies.* Bangor, Gwynedd: Headstart History, 1992.

Luke, Mary. *The Nine Day Queen.* New York: W. Morrow, 1986.

Nichols, John Gough, Esq. The Chronicle of Queen Jane and of Two Years of Queen Mary and Especially of the Rebellion of Sir Thomas Wyat. London: AMS Press, 1850.

Nicolas, Sir Harris. *The Chronology of History.* 2nd Edition. London: Longman, Brown, Green and Longmans, 1838.

Nicholas, Nicolas Harris, Esq. *Literary Remains of Lady Jane Grey.* London: Harding, Triphook and Lepard, 1825.

Petyt. *A Catalogue of the Petyt Library at Skipton.* Yorkshire, Gargrave, England: Coulthurst Trust, 1964.

Plowden, Alison. *Lady Jane Grey & The House of Suffolk.* London: Sidgwick & Jackson, 1985.

Smethwick, John. *Poems by Michael Drayton, Esq.* London: William Stanby, 1630.

Southern, Henry and Nicholas Harris Nicolas. *The Retrospective Review & Historical and Antiquarian Magazine.* London: John Wyat, 1827.

Strype, John. Ecclesiastical Memorials; relating chiefly to religion, and the reformation of it. London England: John Wyat, 1721 and 1733 editions.

—. Memorials of the Most Reverend Father in God, Thomas Cranmer, sometime Lord Archbishop of Canterbury. In three books. London: R. Chiswell, 1694.

Taylor, I.A. *Lady Jane Grey and Her Times.* London: Huchinson & Co., 1908.

SECONDARY SOURCES

Banks, John. *The Tragedy of the Lady Jane Gray.* London: B. Lintott, 1729.

—. *The Innocent Usurper, or the Death of the Lady Jane Grey.* London: R. Bentley, 1694.

Bayley, John Esq. F.S.A. *The History and Antiquities of the Tower of London.* In two volumes. London: T. Cadell, 1821-25.

Beer, Barrett L. *Rebellion and Riot.* Kent, Ohio: The Kent State University Press, 1982.

Bentley, Thomas. The Monvment of Matrones: conteining seven funerall Lamps. London: H. Denham, 1582.

Bullinger, Henry. The Judgement of the Reuerend Father Master Henry Bullinger. Emden: Egidius van der Erve, 1566.

—. *Two Epystles, one of Henry Bullynger.* London: Robert Stoughton within Ludgate, 1548.

Bush, Michael. *The Pilgrimage of Grace. A study of the rebel armies of October 1536.* Manchester. New York: Manchester University Press, 1996.

Byrne, M. St. Clare. *The Letters of King Henry VIII.* London: Cassell and Co. LTD., 1936.

Carte, Thomas. *A General History of England.* 4 Volumes. London, 1752.

Christian. Without a title page, the book has been labeled *Here in this book,* and was written by a Christian. The book resides in the Folger Shakespeare Library. Published in 1554 or 1555.

Collins, Arthur. *Letters and Memorials of State, in the Reigns of Queen Mary, Queen Elizabeth, King James.* London: T. Osborne, 1746.

Dick, William Robertson. *A Short Sketch of the Beauchamp Tower, Tower of London: and also a Guide.* London: Bemros & Sons, 1891.

Dudley, John. *The saying of John late Duke of Northumberland upon the scaffold, at the tyme of his execution. The XXII of Auguste 1553.* London: John Cawood, 1553.

Fabian, Robert. *The Chronicle of Fabian.* London: John Kingston, 1559.

Feckenham, John de. *A notable sermon made within S. Paules church in London.* London: In idibus Roberti Caly, 1555.

Haynes, A.M. Samuel. *A Collection of State Papers from the year 1542 to 1570.* London: W. Bowyer, 1740.

Hibbert, Christopher. *The Virgin Queen.* London: Viking Press, 1990.

Holinshed, Raphael. *The First and Second Volumes of Chronicles, Comprising the Description and History of England, Ireland and Scotland.* London: Henry Denham, 1587.

Horne, Robert. *An Answeare made by Rob. Bishoppe of Wynchester.* London: Henry Wykes, 1566.

Hyrde, Rycharde. *A very frvtfvl and pleasant boke called the Instruction of a Christian Woman.* London, 1547.

Iugge, Richard. *The Prayer of Kynge Edward the syxte.* London: 1553.

Kidgell, John. *An Abridgement of Sr. Richard Bakers Chronicle of the Kings of England.* London: John Kidgell, 1684.

Kiek, Jonathan. *Everybody's Historic London.* London: Quiller Press, 1984.

Loades, David. *John Foxe: An Historical Perspective.* Aldershot; Brookfield, VT: Ashgate, 1999.

Lodge, Edmund, Esq. *Illustrations of British History, Biography, and Manners, in the Reigns of Henry VIII, Edward VI, Mary, Elizabeth, and James I.* London: J. Chidley, 1838.

Loftie, W.J. *Authorised Guide to the Tower of London.* London: for H.M. Stationary Office by Harrison & Son, 1908.

Marshe, T. *A Breuiat Cronicle contaynynge all the kings from brute to this day.* London, 1556.

Mathew, David. *Lady Jane Grey: The setting of the Reign.* London: Eyre Methuen LTD., 1972.

Mears, Kenneth J. *The Tower of London: 900 years of English History.* London: Phaidon, 1988.

Moryfine, Rycharde. *An Introdvction to Wysedome.* London, 1544.

Nichols, John. *A Collection of all the wills now known to be extant of the kings and queens of England.* London England: J. Nichols, 1780.

Pearson, Rev. George. *Remains of Myles Coverdale, Bishop of Exeter.* New York: Johnson Reprint Corp, 1968.

Prescott, Hilda Frances Margaret. *Mary Tudor.* New York: Macmillian, 1953.

Ridley, Jasper. *The Life and Times of Mary Tudor.* London: Weldenfeld and Nicolson, 1973.

Robinson, Rev. Hastings. *Original Letters Relative to the English Reformation, written during the Reigns of King Henry VIII, King Edward VI, and Queen Mary.* New York: Johnson Reprint Corp., 1846.

Rowe, N. Esq. *The Tragedy of Lady Jane Grey.* London: B. Lintott, 1715.

Simon, Linda. *Of Virtue Rare.* Boston: Houghton Mifflin, 1982.

Stevenson, Kenneth. *Nuptial Blessing.* London: Alcuin Club/SPCK, 1982.

Strype, John. *The Life of the Learned Sir John Cheke, Kt. First Instructor, afterwards Secretary of State to King Edward VI.* London: J. Wyat, 1705.

Thurley, Dr. Simon. *The Royal Palaces of Tudor England.* New Haven: Yale University Press, 1993.

Tomson, Laurence. *An answere to certein assertions of M. Fecknam.* London: Henrie Bynneman, 1570.

Townsend, G. Foxe, J. *Acts and Monuments.* London: R.B. Seeley and W. Burnside, 1837-41.

Vance, Marguerite. *Lady Jane Grey — Reluctant Queen.* London, 1952.

Waley, John. *A Table collected of the yeres of our lord God, and of the yeres of the Kings of England*. London, 1567.

Weir, Alison. *The Children of Henry VIII*. New York: Ballantine Books, 1996.

Werdmuller, Otto. *The First Book of Death*. 1555.

—.*A most fruitefull, pithie, and learned treatise, how a Christian man ought to behave himself in the danger of death*. Wesel (?), 1579.

Wright, John. *The Life, Death and Action of the Most Chaste, Learned and Religious Lady, the Lady Jane Grey, daughter to the Duke of Suffolk*. London: G. Eld, 1615.

Young, Edward. *The Force of Religion or, Vanquished Love. Founded upon the Story of the Lady Jane Gray*. Third Edition. London: E. Curll & J. Pemberton, 1715.

Younghusband, Major-General Sir George. *The Tower from Within*. New York: The George H. Doran Co., 1919.

INDEX